The Complete Book
of Terrarium Gardening

THE COMPLETE
BOOK
OF TERRARIUM
GARDENING

Jack Kramer

DRAWINGS BY MICHAEL VALDEZ

Charles Scribner's Sons

New York

For
HELEN VAN PELT WILSON
whose wisdom, friendship,
and advice I always
carry with me

Library of Congress Cataloging in Publication Date
Kramer, Jack, 1927-
   The complete book of terrarium gardening.
   Bibliography: p.
   1. Glass gardens. I. Title.
SB417.K73   635.9'8   73-17253
ISBN 0-684-13703-8

ACKNOWLEDGMENTS

I wish to thank (once again) my photographer Matthew Barr who willingly and without ever complaining shot and reshot photos of various terrariums—the best shown in this book. To Podesta-Baldocchi Inc. of San Francisco, California I offer my appreciation for allowing us to photograph on their premises the handsome Victorian leaded glass cases. Richard Lee, designer of the attractive stained glass terrariums in this book also deserves special mention for his fine cooperation.

Les Cunning, a long time friend, spent several of his weekends to create terrarium arrangements with me and to him I owe a special vote of thanks. Finally, I want to offer my deep gratitude to Louis Christen Jr. of Christen, Inc. of St. Louis, Missouri, who several years ago realized the beauty of terrariums and my love for them and always gave me great encouragement and advice.

AUTHOR'S NOTE

In 1967 I was forced by circumstances to live in a small apartment in Chicago, Illinois. There was little space for indoor gardening (none for outdoor gardening), yet I knew I had to work with plants in some way or I would be miserable. I started growing small plants in glass containers; subsequently, my book *Gardens Under Glass* (Simon & Schuster) was published in 1969. It was the first book on the subject published in the United States in over a quarter of a century.

At the time there was little interest in diminutive gardens that brought nature into my small apartment. But, fascinated, I continued to do terrarium gardening. As time went on, the public too, became beguiled with this hobby. The idea of having a total environment—a natural ecosystem of plants, air, soil and moisture—in the confines of a protected container appealed to people. In 1971 terrariums started to appear in hobby and florist shops and nurseries and by 1972, growing small plants in jars, jugs, and bowls had become a popular pastime and the legion of followers grows daily.

My idea of growing plants in terrariums certainly wasn't original; it had been done over a century before in England when ferns and all kinds of decorative plants were grown in parlor cases.

Today the idea of growing plants in transparent containers is so popular that there is hardly a person who does not know what a terrarium is. The popularity of terrariums is justly deserved for there is no better way to keep, grow, and admire plants at home. This book is a record of my many years with small plants in terrariums of all kinds. It has been a fascinating and ever-interesting kind of gardening for me, and I hope it appeals to you in the same way.

Jack Kramer

CONTENTS

The Complete Book
of Terrarium Gardening

Parlor cases of Victorian era were elaborately designed and used as much for housing small landscapes as for their decorative appeal.

1

TERRARIUM GARDENING

The word terrarium derives from *terra* (earth) and *ium* (with). Whether in plastic spheres or glass globes, in parlor cases or under domes, in bottles or jugs, terrariums are essentially a group of small plants in soil inside a transparent container. The containers are generally covered but may be partially open, as with bubble bowls.

In 1836 Dr. Nathaniel Bagshaw Ward, a London physician, started what we today call terrariums: a glass case for growing plants. Ward was trying to hatch a moth chrysalis in a soil-filled covered bottle when he discovered small ferns growing in the soil. The moisture from the soil had caused condensation to form on the inside of the glass; the water dropped in rivulets back to the soil.

Ward himself hinted that his discovery was not original; he had simply improved a case used for the transport of plants by sea that John Ellis, a London merchant and naturalist, had perfected in 1771. And in 1782 J. E. Smith gave a lecture at Edinburgh; he mentioned that he had kept specimens fresh in jars of water set inside larger jars. The Scottish botanist A. A. Maconochie showed in 1825 that plants live better in glass containers; his work was based on experiments of the Swiss scientist de Saussure in 1780. However, Ward, unlike his predecessors, published his findings, and thus it is with Ward that we associate closed glass cases for plants.

In the early 1840's the Wardian case was not only ideal for growing plants but also for transporting plants on long sea voyages from foreign lands. Plants of all kinds, including orchids and ferns, were a booming business. The English, natural plant lovers, led the way in the pursuit of exotic plants and flowers to dazzle guests in elaborate and costly greenhouses. And in the 1850s, when the glass

3

tax was repealed and glass became available to more people, the demand for plants was incredible. In a short time Wardian cases appeared as decorative accents in homes to house both small and large plants. Ultimately, a host of imitators designed cases fashioned from the Wardian concept for ornamental use in interiors. Once the simple principle was revealed, there was a terrarium madness. Some terrariums, or parlor cases as they were called, were intricately designed, with small boilers and water drains, and one case was more elaborate than the next. In Germany, glass cases were used for propagating precious seeds and for small animal life. In France and Russia, the terrariums were used as homes for natural lilliputian

This old terrarium was well planted and even had a temperature gauge (right corner). Ferns and all kinds of plants thrived in such cases.

THE WOODLAND GARDEN

A Selaginella

B Cyclamen

C Cyrtomium falcatum

D Tree Branch

E Trailing Arbutus

F Moss

G Maranta massangeana

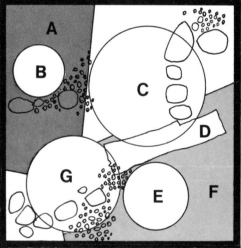

THE TROPICAL GARDEN

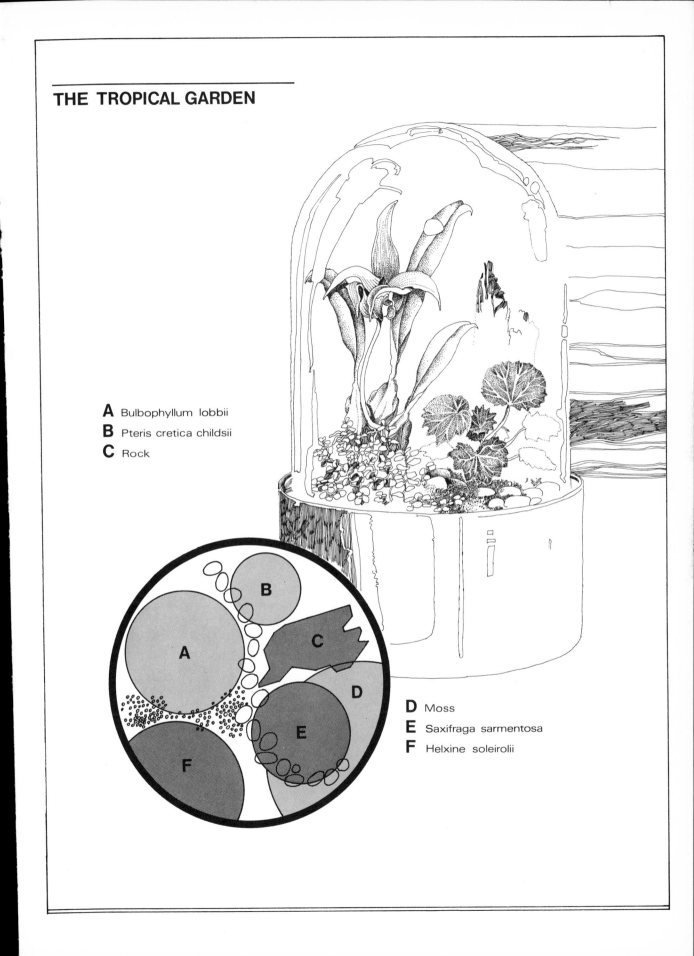

A Bulbophyllum lobbii
B Pteris cretica childsii
C Rock

D Moss
E Saxifraga sarmentosa
F Helxine soleirolii

A handsome terrarium with an Oriental motif is featured in this photo. Doors opened for easy access to plants.

THE DESERT GARDEN

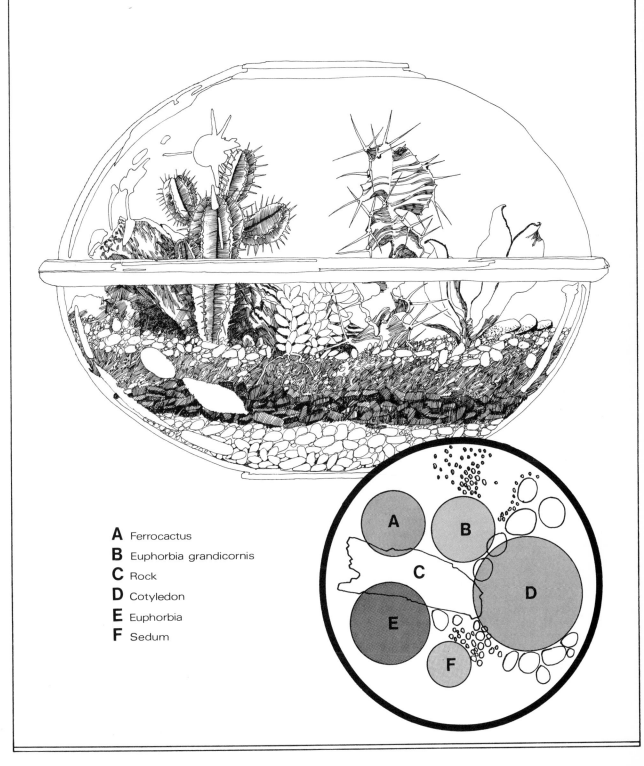

A Ferrocactus
B Euphorbia grandicornis
C Rock
D Cotyledon
E Euphorbia
F Sedum

abilities, and, like the Japanese art of bonsai or saikei (making miniature scenes of nature), you create the work—the resulting picture can be as beautiful as you want it to be. The tiny landscape may be reminiscent of a woodland garden or as verdant as a tropical jungle. The garden may simulate a bog habitat (a very interesting ecosystem) or be a desert scene. Use nature as your guide in assembling your tiny gardens.

The plastic sphere is today's popular terrarium and makes a fine appointment for any room. This one houses small pileas and ground covers. (Photo by Matthew Barr)

TERRARIUM CONTAINERS

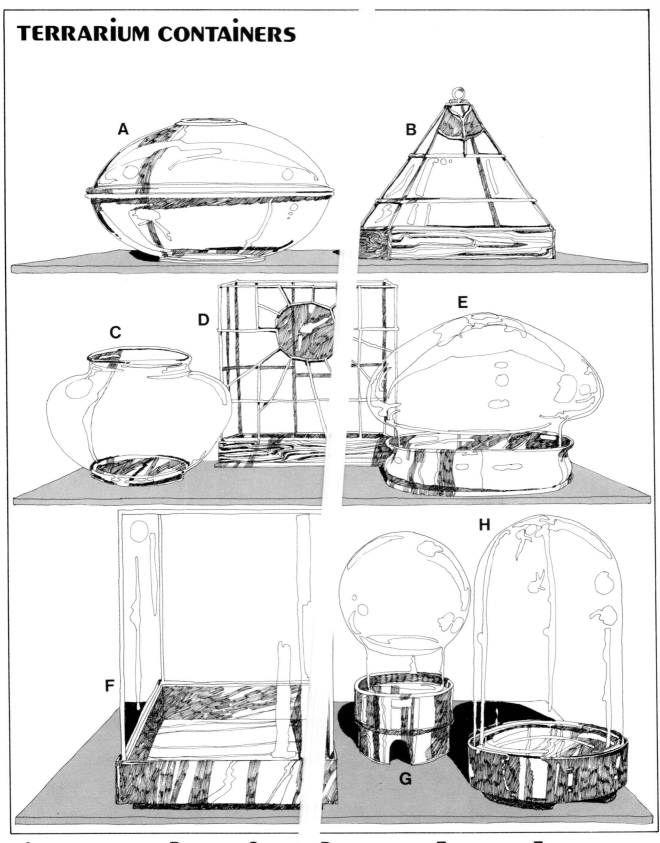

A EGG (TERRA-SPHERE); **B** PYRAMID; **C** CARBO̶ **D** LEADED GLASS; **E** MUSHROOM; **F** SQUARE;
G GLOBE; **H** DOME

For many years aquariums were used as housings for woodland landscapes such as this. The plants grown were native subjects and ferns. (Photo by author)

10, 15, or 20 gallons. With a suitable glass top these make fine terrariums for larger plants. Standard-sized tanks, in inches, are

LENGTH	WIDTH	DEPTH
12	6	6
14	8	8
18	10	10
24	12	12
36	12	12

In addition to the standard glass aquariums, all-glass housings without angle posts are now available; the sides are glued together with strong epoxies. This type of construction allows a clear picture of the garden without vertical obstructions.

DOMES: The glass d⋯e, a product of the Victorian fern craze, is
highly elegant and a⋯ a special note to any area. When I first
started terrarium gard⋯ng, buying commercial domes was almost
impossible. I remembe⋯ aveling 40 miles to the outskirts of Chicago
to find my first one; t⋯ dealer was the only manufacturer we had
in the entire city. To⋯ glass domes of many sizes are sold at nurseries. The average do⋯ is 10 × 16 inches high and deserves special
planting. Restraint mu⋯ e exercised: too many plants spoil the picture, and too few mak⋯ e scene sparse.

Generally, the dome⋯old separately. You must supply the planting dish, but this is n⋯ifficult. For example, you will find many
suitable dishes in salvag⋯ ores. Remember that the diameters of the
glass dome and the dis⋯ ust match so the dome rests on the dish.

*Domes for terrariums w⋯ difficult to find at one time; this glass dome
originally was used to pr⋯ t a stuffed bird. The dish was found in a sal-
vage shop. (Photo by aut⋯)*

Recently some kits with the dish and dome and stones, soil, and so forth have been marketed; they are somewhat expensive but charming.

There is now a mushroom-shaped dome sold with dish and supplies on the market. The mushroom part of the dome is almost 18 inches across; the neck is about 10 inches. I have found that planting is somewhat tricky because you must select plants that naturally have long stems or trunks and clusters of leaves. Palmlike plants are the answer. Like the glass dome, the mushroom terrarium is impressive and offers limitless planting arrangements.

BOTTLES: A terrarium can also be an attractive bottle that would otherwise be thrown away. If the bottle is large enough, it can be used as is, like the old ship-in-the-bottle mantlepiece motif. Special tools are needed for bottle gardens, but the results are well worth the effort. By the way, for a self-sustaining terrarium, the larger the container the better the chance of achieving the balance necessary to make the terrarium work on its own. A 3-gallon size is ideal, although I have planted smaller bottles with some success.

So far I have seen only one bottle garden kit at suppliers; it includes a 3-gallon water-type bottle and all necessary planting tools and materials: soil, gravel, and charcoal (you supply the plants). The bottle is not overly dramatic, and other shapes such as the carboy are more unique, but there is an advantage in that you have everything at hand without having to shop in five places for materials. Once the bottle is either vertically or horizontally planted (it comes with wooden stands), you will find that the kit is certainly a worthwhile investment.

When shopping for your own bottles remember that (1) the shape of the bottle must be handsome, (2) there must be sufficient space for plants, (3) the neck of the bottle should be at least 1 inch in diameter, and (4) the glass should be transparent. Having done bottle gardening for years, I find the round or globular shapes the best for planting because they are attractive and have sufficient growing space. Tall rectangular bottles are difficult to plant and

This five-gallon water bottle makes a fine terrarium; there is ample space for plants and balance of elements is good. (Photo by author)

can accommodate only a few plants. Ideally the bottle should be at least 10 inches in diameter and 12 inches high. In addition to a bottle's shape and size, consider its color. Even clear glass comes in different tints, ranging from blue-green to crystal clear. Avoid colored bottles—blue, amber, green.

A good source of unusual bottles is a chemist supply house (listed in the Yellow Pages under "Scientific Glassware"). Flasks and beakers of various sizes make stunning containers for diminutive gardens.

With a bottle cutter you can now use two bottles to make one. For example, cut one bottle 3 inches from the bottom. Cut the second jug as close to the bottom as possible. Plant the first bottle with soil and plants, and then merely place the top half of the second jug on top. Seal the segments with epoxy. Or simply use the bottom half with a piece of glass over it as a terrarium.

OTHERS: You can also find suitable glass containers for plants in the glassware department of stores or boutiques. Glass salad or punch bowls are ideal if you want unique terrariums, although you will have to have a top fashioned for the greenhouse at a glass store. (Circular glass tops of 3/16-inch glass are ideal). Apothecary jars of various sizes and designs are also available at florist shops, and of course glass water bottles, vinegar jars, peanut butter jars, cookie jars, and glass or plastic globes used for lighting fixtures are all part of the terrarium picture.

Plastic Containers

SPHERE-TYPE: These can be plastic or glass; either way the sphere-type terrarium is ideal for plants because it allows ample planting room (the top of the sphere nests into the bottom half) and is not cumbersome. The sphere measures 12 or 14 inches across and is easy to plant. There are several types of plastic available, some clearer than others. This degree of transparency is what you should be concerned about when purchasing terrariums. The heavier and harder the plastic, the longer it will last, and the clearer the material, the better you can see through it. There are various grades and types of plastic, so be alert when purchasing terrariums made of it.

TRAPEZOID-TYPE: The trapezoid-shaped plastic terrarium is another new product. This is essentially a box set on a box, approximately 10 × 16 inches. The design is simple and attractive and, like the sphere, easy to plant. The horizontal design allows the hobbyist to create long narrow greeneries rather than restricting himself to the circular or round design.

Nurseries now sell plastic terrariums. These are designed and shaped so that there is ample horizontal planting space. Some have stands to elevate the garden scene. (Photo by Matthew Barr)

AQUARIUMS: As mentioned, glass has been the standard material for aquariums for decades, but the newer plastics deserve consideration. They are now available in hexagonal and bowed shapes and are highly attractive. Plastic aquariums are generally large, about 24 inches long, or, in the case of the hexagonal container, 36 inches high, which allows you to grow tall plants. There are no posts or hardware to obstruct viewing. Some have epoxied tops, but with others you may have to have tops fitted and cut. The plastic cases are generally expensive, but they are unique and can certainly be used to make stellar miniature gardens.

Years ago plastic was grayish in color and invariably yellowed. Today's plastics are much clearer and do not yellow, so they are well worth the money. They do, however, scratch, so handle carefully. If you do decide on a large plastic terrarium, be sure it is ¼ inch thick so it can hold the weight of the soil, and be sure it is reasonably transparent. There is nothing more frustrating than planting a beautiful lilliputian garden and then not being able to see it.

In these larger containers you can use tree-like plants and create vivid scenes with stones and ledges, gravel and pebbles. These terrariums are not as charming as the smaller ones, but they are more impressive to the viewer because they are a total ecosystems. Also, because of the additional space, planning the garden design is increasingly challenging, and once established the garden is enjoyable.

A larger terrarium requires suitable supports—a table, desk, or individual stand—for proper displaying. The support should be strong. A 24-gallon terrarium filled with stones and plants is heavy, so assemble it where you want it to be rather than trying to carry it planted to a designated place. You will not only hurt yourself, but it is possible that the bottom of the terrarium will tear loose.

Special Terrariums

HANGING: I have seen only one type of commercial hanging terrarium (plastic bubble bowl with top and bottom to form a globe), but no doubt more designs will be available soon. The prin-

Terrariums for hanging are also available; this globe has two halves with a small air space in between to provide ventilation in the garden. The globe is suspended with wire. (Photo by Don Worth)

ciple of the hanging terrarium is a good one: Plants are always on display and in an enviable position to get light. Furthermore, the hanging terrarium allows you to use otherwise wasted space near windows. Once elevated the greenery takes on a new aspect, with infinitely appealing results.

THE HANGING FERNERY

A Pteris cretica childsii
B Rock
C Davallia fejeensis
D Selaginella
E Pteris ensiformis

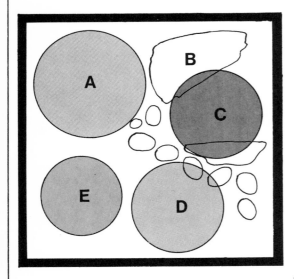

For my hanging terrariums I have used plastic or blown-glass light fixtures and adapted them to my use. With one of them I had to insert a glass bottom, a simple procedure of merely putting in a glass circle and covering it with soil. I made the other hanging terrarium by eliminating the light fixture hardware from the center of the globe and gluing a dish to the bottom opening.

Another recent innovation is making hanging containers from bottles. With a bottle-cutting kit you can cut bottles midway or lower and use the bottom of the bottle in a macramé or string sling. (Be sure to sand the cut edges to avoid cutting yourself before planting the terrarium.)

Elaborate leaded glass terrariums are highly decorative and provide a living green scene for any room. Ivy, ferns, agloanema, and ground covers combine to create a stunning lilliputian landscape. (Photo by Matthew Barr)

LEADED GLASS: Leaded glass has become popular again and it is indeed handsome when used as a small terrarium. I have seen these terrariums designed like fern cases in florists' shops. Some are dome, rectangular, or pyramidal in shape. You can also have a local crafts-man make a case especially to your design and tastes; the cost will be high, but the results will be stunning. Or you can buy a leaded-glass terrarium kit and put it together yourself by using a soldering iron. In any event, be sure what you get is really lead glass channel and not metallic sheet that wraps around glass sections. This is slip-

With Oriental character, this six-sided terrarium of leaded glass design is very handsome. The accent plant is pothos. (Photo by Matthew Barr)

shod because eventually the foil peels away from the glass. The leaded-glass case brimming with colorful plants is an elegant addition to any room. But inspect these terrariums closely to be sure they are made properly, or, if you make them yourself, use the best materials.

WALL UNITS: Wall units of curved glass in wood frames are also available. These very tiny gardens are charming, but they do not have ample space to really establish an ecosystem, so they will not sustain plant life for a long time. Still, for their beauty they are worth the money and will last several months, if not years.

No matter what kind of special case you have made or buy or make yourself, be sure it has an ample opening so you can plant it easily.

3

PRINCIPLES OF
TERRARIUM GARDENING

Terrarium gardens are ideal for the indoor gardener not only because they make it easy to grow plants, but because they are attractive almost any place. And perhaps most important is the fact that these small greeneries are self-sustaining. Watering plants (generally a dilemma for many people) becomes hardly any problem. In the closed case, watering is done by nature. In partially opened terrariums, some watering is necessary. Temperature is another thing you need not worry about, for in protected containers, temperatures do not fluctuate abruptly. Furthermore, plants in transparent cases are protected against insects (as a rule) and once set up, terrariums are simple to care for; all that is really needed is grooming of plants and lifting the lid or cover so some air can circulate within the garden. Also, plants in terrariums get plenty of humidity; the natural cycle supplies humidity. Also a factor, and a vital one that is generally overlooked, is that terrariums must be balanced to sustain plant life. There must be enough space to sustain the right balance of air, moisture, humidity, plants, and soil.

General Care

Plants in terrariums, as mentioned, will make their own water. Indeed, many times the soil may become too soggy and if you see moisture on the inside of the terrarium (you cannot see the plants) remove the lid or stopper a few hours each day.

Closed cases will not need water for months. In fact, many can go years without moisture. Partially opened containers (bubble bowls, bottles), may need an occasional watering, perhaps once a month, depending on the size of the terrarium. If you do think your

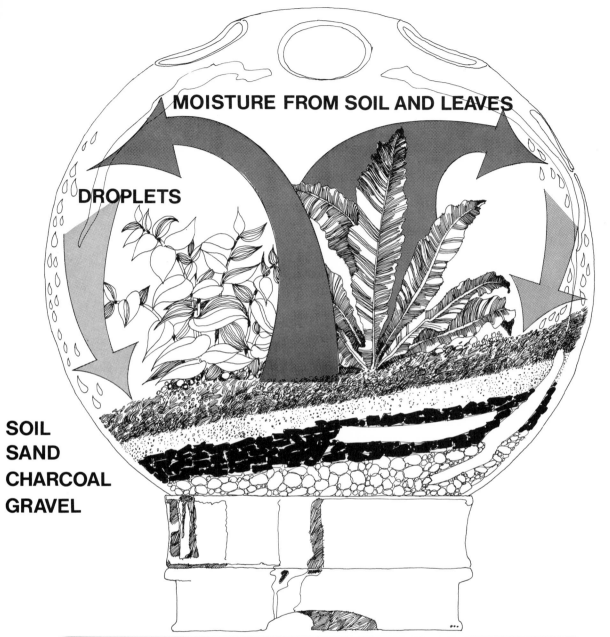

MOISTURE FROM SOIL AND LEAVES

DROPLETS

SOIL
SAND
CHARCOAL
GRAVEL

principle of a terrarium

Moisture from leaves and soil condenses on glass and runs back into soil.

The closeup photo shows condensation on the inside of the terrarium which runs down into the soil. The moisture is provided by the leaves and the cycle repeats itself continuously so a closed terrarium never needs water. (Photos by Don Worth)

terrarium needs water (when soil is dry to the touch), do not just dump water into it or you will make a mess. Mud splatters quickly, and mars glass, and may dislodge plants from their places. Use a gentle stream of water poured down the sides of the terrarium so it just trickles into the soil. (Use room temperature water.)

Never over-water. Remember that terrariums do not have drainage holes, so too much water, even if you have a charcoal-gravel base soil, can turn soil soggy and sour, which will harm plants. If by chance you err and get too much water in the garden, use a basting tube (sold at kitchen and hardware stores) to remove some of the excess water. Never tilt or lean a terrarium to remove water because plants and soil will tilt too; you will have ruined your garden.

Many gardeners are inclined to believe that all plants must be given additional fertilizers. This is incorrect. Plants in large pots that quickly deplete soil of nutrients need some feeding, but small plants in terrariums do not need feeding at all. Indeed, additional fertilizers will create toxic salts that can kill plants. Remember too, that you want your plants to stay small and not grow rapidly, so feeding is hardly necessary.

Light is essential to plants; without it they do not grow. However, with plants in closed terrariums sunlight can mean death to them. Heat accumulates within the container and bakes plants. Therefore, put your tiny garden in a bright place, but not in direct noonday sun. For the most part, the woodland and bog recreated scenes do just fine in a somewhat north or west exposure. The desert or tropical garden will tolerate more light, perhaps a few hours of late afternoon sun. Remember that terrariums are portable so you can move the garden if there is too much light or not enough brightness for plants.

How The Terrarium Works

The manufacturing process of plants includes using carbon dioxide from the air and releasing oxygen. But a plant also reverses the process; that is, it uses oxygen, frees carbon dioxide, and uses organic materials in a process known as respiration. When the temperature is high, evaporation of the moisture from leaves condenses on the walls inside the terrarium. The water collects in droplets and runs down in rivulets back to the soil, and the cycle goes on and on.

This natural cycle always provides humidity and moisture, two

Woodland plants in this plastic terrarium could not live on a window sill. However, here they thrive in their protected environment—a diminutive natural habitat. (Photo by author)

vital factors that influence good plant growth. But a terrarium must be large enough so this cycle can function. Thus, I repeat: balance is the key—a proper balance of air, light, humidity, moisture, plants, and soil.

When plants are placed at windows in our homes they suffer from lack of humidity for most homes (unless equipped with humidifiers) have low humidity. So, generally, house plants have a tough time growing. But this is not so in terrariums. As explained, healthy plants transpire through their leaves; if the air around them is dry, the moisture given off by the leaves evaporates quickly. If the room is extremely dry, a pot plant gives off more water than it can spare and the plant wilts. In a glass case—bottle, sphere, et cetera —the moisture given off by the leaves is conserved, remaining in the air as vapor within the transparent minigarden or condensing on the soil. This, coupled with the vapor rising from the soil, provides an evenly moist atmosphere which is essential for good plant growth.

Why It Works

Why does the plant in a terrarium grow lavishly while a plant of the same kind at a window will die in a few months? One reason is that, for the most part, terrarium plants are tropical in nature and thus thrive on the warmth and humidity supplied by the closed case. Another reason why terrariums work is that plants in groups are natural. The little ecosystem of earth, light, moisture, and plants make a complete scene; a plant in a pot at a window is out of its element. (Frank McGee of the TODAY Show helped me make this discovery when he asked why terrariums are so popular. He too felt that the attractiveness of the plants grouped together was the difference—not the only one—the reason most people migrate to terrarium growing.)

Another aspect to consider is that the sheet of glass or plastic that separates your green world from the real world puts your plants on display; they resemble store windows, and everyone enjoys looking at store windows. Like a television set with its glass pane, a mirror, or any glass object, the eye is attracted to it instantly. And, too, terrariums work because it is easy to remedy mistakes in planting (by replacing a plant), or if an arrangement does not suit you, you can simply change it by removing the lid. Also to be considered is miniaturization: miniature objects fascinate all people, for example small dolls, tiny furniture, and scale model railroads. A terrarium works because of its smallness; it intrigues everyone who views it.

Advantages

Pot plants are sometimes a problem to place in a home, and even with clay saucers there is water stain on wood. With glass or plastic terrariums, water stain is eliminated, and the garden can be placed anywhere where a living green accent is needed. For example, the elegant apothecary jar resplendent with lacy ferns can grace a living room. The more conventional plastic sphere filled with glowing green mosses can be on a bedroom windowsill, and the Victorian dome garden can accent a coffee table or desk. Remember that terrariums are *portable* gardens you can move about at will. In early morning beads of condensation sparkle like diamonds, and plants appear as if they are in the forest. In the evening, shadows and light highlight leaves and flowers in special beauty. Here plants are as they should be, rather than out of place at a window.

A handsome terrarium such as this can be placed anywhere in the home for decoration. It does not need to be, nor should it be at a window sill. (Photo by Matthew Barr)

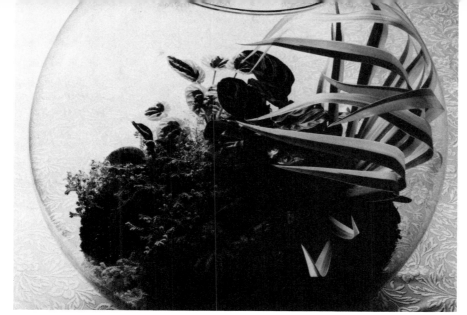

Maranta, the accent plant in this bubble bowl, is difficult to grow as a house plant. However, in a terrarium it does very well because it gets ample humidity, often lacking in homes. (Photo by Don Worth)

Pot plants, too, after a time, get straggly—even well-grown ones —and are thwarted by the window glass. Plants press against windows and become ungainly and unsightly. Even the well-planned window garden must be limited to a straight line of pot plants. This is hardly aesthetically pleasing, and too, there may be the accident when a pot falls to the floor.

Another advantage of terrariums is the protection they offer plants from dust and soot. Plants breathe through tiny pores in their leaves, and if these are choked, as they are apt to be from natural pollution in the home, the merest film of dust on foliage can lead to an unhealthy plant. In their glass cases, plants are also protected against the harmful effects of tobacco smoke or gas fumes. Fumes unnoticeable to human beings can be injurious to plants. Even exhaust fumes from cars driving down the street adjacent to your home could cause some fragile plants to wilt at windows, but not when they are in their miniature greenhouses.

A final advantage is that you can grow any kind of plant you want—there are few restrictions. Even difficult carnivorous plants (Venus fly trap, sundew) will respond in the protected environment of a glass case. Woodland native plants from New York can grow in California, and California tropicals can thrive in Chicago.

4

GETTING STARTED— THE BASICS

For many kinds of gardening you need elaborate equipment and supplies to be successful. But when you garden in terrariums you avoid such costs and still get results that are just as rewarding. If you are frugal, even the container may be free: an empty household jar or water bottle. And the amount of soil, charcoal, and gravel used to sustain your little garden is small, no more than you would probably use for a large pot plant. The only other necessary things you will need to bring to a garden indoors are a good sense of planting design, your fingers, and a basic love of plants.

Tools

If you are planting wide-mouthed bowls and jars, you can forget about tools—you just will not need them; deft fingers and experience are prerequisites. For narrow-neck bottle gardening you will need a plastic funnel (25 cents), a long-handled spoon, a few dowel sticks, and a pickup tool (99 cents at most hardware stores). However, you can even make your own pickup tool: fashion a wire loop from an old coat hanger, then insert plants in place in narrow-mouthed bottles. To clean bottles of plant debris use an X-acto knife (20 cents), and an artist's brush (20 cents, available at art stores). These tools can be taped to dowel sticks, or even cheaper, a paper clip curved and taped to a dowel stick will enable you to help remove faded flowers and leaves from terrariums.

Any other tool you will buy will be a luxury, not a necessity. I worked for years on terrariums with household items and still do, even when I give TV or lecture demonstrations.

tools

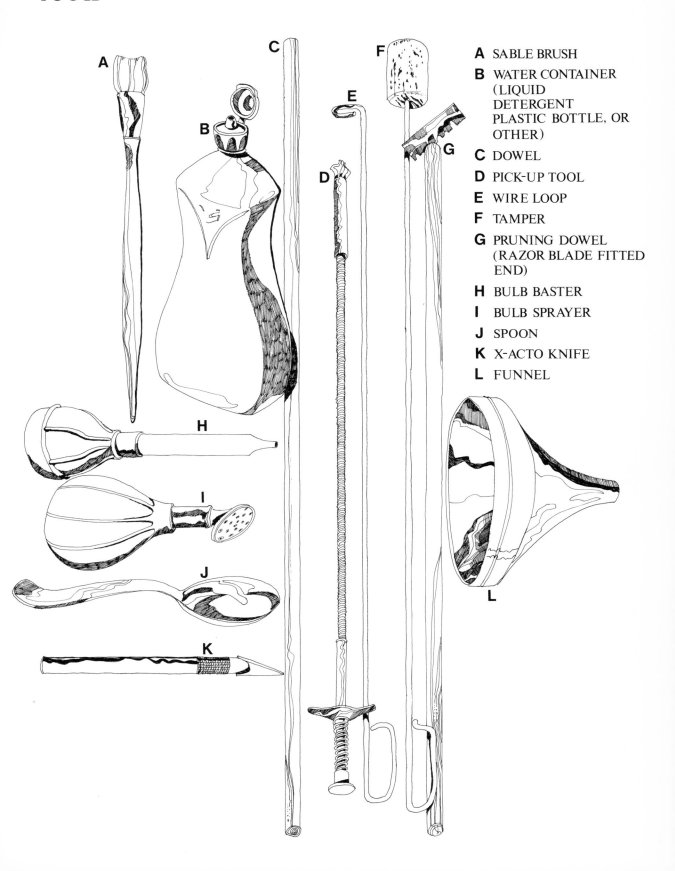

A SABLE BRUSH

B WATER CONTAINER
(LIQUID
DETERGENT
PLASTIC BOTTLE, OR
OTHER)

C DOWEL

D PICK-UP TOOL

E WIRE LOOP

F TAMPER

G PRUNING DOWEL
(RAZOR BLADE FITTED
END)

H BULB BASTER

I BULB SPRAYER

J SPOON

K X-ACTO KNIFE

L FUNNEL

Soil

Soil is a necessary ingredient for terrariums. Packaged soils designated as house plant soil are fine. (Generally a one dollar package is all that is needed.) Certain cacti and succulents will require some sand added to the regular soil, and orchids and bromeliads will require small-grade fir bark (also sold in tidy sacks at suppliers).

Some plants, however, do need a richer soil than what is found in packages. If you are a perfectionist, you might want to make your own soil mix; I suggest a mixture of 1 part sand, 1 part topsoil, and 1 part leaf mold or humus. A somewhat richer soil for plants such as begonias and some gesneriads would be 2 parts topsoil, 1 part sand, and 1 part leaf mold. There are many different soil mixes.

Most terrariums do not have drainage holes. Water-logged soil

Gravel, charcoal, soil, rocks for planting, a plastic sphere are shown here. Small plants taken from their pots will make the garden. (Photo by Matthew Barr)

This closeup shot shows small rocks and gravel used as finishing accessories in this diminutive landscape. (Photo by Matthew Barr)

If you look closely at this bottle garden you can see the layers of charcoal and gravel at the bottom of the container. This garden is two years old and ready for replanting. It had never been watered. (Photo by author)

can mean death to plants, so you want a well-aerated, nutritious, spongy soil. Air and water must circulate readily through the soil or you will have a compacted dry soil that cannot support plants for long. Be sure that whatever soil you use is porous and has good tilth (texture). Feel it with your hands: a good soil feels mealy, like a well-done baked potato. Avoid soilless or peatlike mixtures as growing mediums because they have no nutrients. Constant feeding will then be necessary, which is always a chore rather than a pleasure.

Charcoal

Charcoal is another necessary item in the terrarium. By its chemical nature, charcoal helps keep the soil sweet and can mean the difference between a healthy little garden and a sick one. You can use charcoal from your fireplace, or buy it in tidy sacks or boxes from aquarium stores.

Gravel

Gravel is necessary in terrariums because it prevents water-logged soil. A thin layer of gravel acts like a drain: the water spreads laterally and is distributed and evaporates on the many surfaces of the gravel rather than falling to the bottom of the soil bed. Without gravel, water immediately runs to the bottom of the soil, resulting eventually in a stagnant soil. Do *not* under any condition omit the gravel in terrariums, unless containers have drainage holes. Use ⅛-inch crushed gravel. This is neither too small nor too large and has many surfaces. Pea gravel will not work because it is round and smooth; water runs off it.

Years ago it was the popular custom to line terrariums with sphagnum moss. Actually, the moss liner is not needed by plants, and indeed, the natural tendency of the material to hold water can hinder plant growth.

Finishing Touches

The addition of small figurines and carved stone sculptures to terrariums can help establish a scene and add dimension. The usual ceramic and plastic figurines are hardly tasteful in tiny gardens, but the newer pieces do have merit. They are finely detailed and can add great charm to the garden when used with discretion.

Colored stone and gravel are finishing touches that can make an ordinary garden extraordinary. Oval and rounded Japanese black cobbles, all the same size and meticulously placed, add beauty to a

A closeup view showing the use of rocks and stones in this garden as finishing touches. (Photo by Matthew Barr)

This completed terrarium is in the author's dining area. Ground covers and small Japanese white stones were used as special accents. The plants left to right are: a miniature orchid, a small rex begonia, fern, and pilea. (Photo by Matthew Barr)

scene. Small areas of colored gravel used as paths or islands are also handsome attractions and can certainly be part of the terrarium picture provided they fit into the garden. Here is where the sense of design is paramount; it is not how much you put in but what you leave out that makes the total landscape in glass attractive.

I think small rocks and stones used as ledges are other necessary elements for fashioning a fine terrarium. Twigs and bark can also be used to help simulate the natural scene (which in essence is what we are trying to do). The rock ledges should be integral parts of the landscape, the soil built around them with planting pockets. Tufa rock is excellent and can be fashioned with a knife. To simulate ledges you can cement thin slabs of rock together. Tiny walking ferns and cliffbrakes are delightful in such a situation.

The terrarium creation that is a combination of plants and soil, gravel and stone, rock ledges, and interesting pieces of wood is a work of art, and takes infinite patience and experience. But once the finished product graces a table or desk it is indeed a joy to see. The craftsman's and plantsman's arts have been combined with nature to fashion a lovely garden.

5

TERRARIUM PLANTS: FOLIAGE AND FLOWERING

There is a wide variety of terrarium plants, and new ones are introduced frequently. Plant suppliers have responded to the demand for glass-garden beauty with some rare, small plants that until recently were not available. For example, hypoestes, a small plant with oval green leaves dotted yellow, has appeared at Woolworths in the last few months. I haven't seen this plant available for years.

Although almost any foliage or flowering plant can be grown under glass, miniatures are best because they grow slowly, and even at maturity most do not outgrow the average terrarium. Dwarf plants too, are excellent, and seedlings of mature plants can be used, but remember that in time they will become big plants. Collectors' plants like African violets and orchids can be infinitely charming in terrariums, as can small begonias, which glisten like jewels in transparent containers.

Miniature and Small House Plants

Within many plant families there are miniatures, small plants that never grow more than 12 inches. Miniatures are in the Gesneriad family—African violets, episcias—and also in the Begonia clan, with more than 50 kinds. Some true miniature geraniums never grow more than 8 inches tall. Because of their colorful flowers and foliage, Geraniums are worth your attention, although they may not be as easy to grow as some other house plants.

In the Peperomia family there are many small plants too, with a wide variety of leaf color and size. Pileas are also favorite terrarium subjects. There are twenty different peperomias and twelve pileas

ACORUS GRAMINEUS

HEDERA HELIX

CAMPTOSORUS RHYZOPHYLLUS

SMALL PLANTS

(although not all true miniatures) available from suppliers. The vast Orchid family contains thousands of little plants, some like *Masdevallia lilliputana* only 1-inch high, and tiny desert cacti with their bizarre shapes are always intriguing. *Sinningia pusillus*, a Gesneriad, bears delightful funnel-shaped flowers, and plants are only 1 inch; the colorful blooms under glass brighten the dreariest morning. So there are a great many miniature or small plants you can choose from to create your garden under glass.

Miniature Trees

In addition to small house plants, there are bonsai-type trees—spruce and cedar, for example—that you can grow in open terrariums. These beautiful evergreens can create total nature scenes that are most appealing. Some are less than 10 inches tall at 10 years and are charming replicas of hardy types found in outdoor gardens. Some do not grow more than 1 inch a year and are as bright and colorful in winter as in summer. However, bonsai plants need good air circulation and clipping and trimming, so keep them in open containers, as previously mentioned.

Miniature house plants and trees rarely are expensive; even lilliputian orchids cost no more than three dollars. Thus a complete terrarium with several plants need not cost much, and it will always return a wealth of beauty indoors.

For simplicity we have classified plants either as foliage or flowering in the following lists. Miniatures (dwarfs or very small plants) are denoted by an asterisk. Ferns, native plants, ground covers, and mosses are discussed in the next chapter. The letters S, M, or L after the description of a plant denote "small," "medium," or "large." (See Appendix A for complete list of plants). The letters W, B, D, or T indicate whether plants are ideal for woodland, bog, desert, or tropical gardens (see Appendix B).

List of Foliage Plants

Acorus gramineus pusillus (sweet flag)   Tufted, grassy leaves; 2 to 3 inches high. Excellent terrarium plant. S; W

Adromischus clavifolius   Small, with club-shaped leaves flecked with reddish marks. S; D

A. maculatus (calico hearts)   Thick gray-green flat leaves spotted with brown; can bloom in terrariums. Flowers are red-tipped. S; D

Aglaonema commutatum (Chinese evergreen)   Dark green leaves with silver markings; slow growing. M; T

A. pictum   One of the best foliage plants, with blue-green leaves splashed with silver. Somewhat large, but can be trimmed to desired shape and size. M; T

Aloe brevifolia variegata   Rarely grows over 5 inches in diameter; beautiful vertically striped leaves laced with lines of white. S; D

Alternanthera bettzichiana   Bright miniature with yellow, pink, red, and green foliage. Group a few of these in one area for some concentrated color. S; T

Anthurium scherzerianum (flamingo plant)   Attractive green leaves; red shiny bracts. M; T

Astrophytum myriostigma (bishop's cap)   This old favorite is a spineless odd plant shaped like a bishop's hood. S; D

Bambusa nana (miniature bamboo)   Grassy plant that needs severe pruning; use only a few shoots. M; T

Caladium A group with many varieties well-suited to diminutive landscapes. Try C. *humboldtii*—small deep-green leaves marked with silver; 'Little Rascal'—lance-shaped wine-red foliage; or 'Twilight'—flaming pink leaves netted with green. These plants may die in winter; if so, lift them from the garden. M; T

Calathea bachemiana Not really a miniature but a lush plant with velvety gray-green leaves edged with dark green. S, W. Also handsome is the dwarf C. *picturata argentea*, with silver leaves etched in dark green. S; T

Ceropegia cafforum (string of hearts) A climber, with dark-green leaves, that are red underneath. Another dainty species is C. *woodii* (rosary vine), with heart-shaped blue-green foliage with silver veins. M; D

Chamaedorea elegans (bamboo balm) Lovely dwarf palm with bright green fronds. L; T

Chamaeranthemum igneum Tropical creeper with velvety bronze-brown leaves and pink veins. M; T

Chlorophytum bichetii (spider plant) Rosettes of lovely green grassy leaves with white stripes. M; T

Cleistocactus strausii Spiny columnar cactus. L; D

Codiaeum variegatum pictum (croton) Bushy plant that needs pruning to keep it small. Has bright-green leaves spotted with yellow. Use in open terrariums. L; T

*Cotyledon Small succulent plants; leaves leathery, light green or green. S; D

Crassula cooperi Three-inch leathery leaved plant. S; D

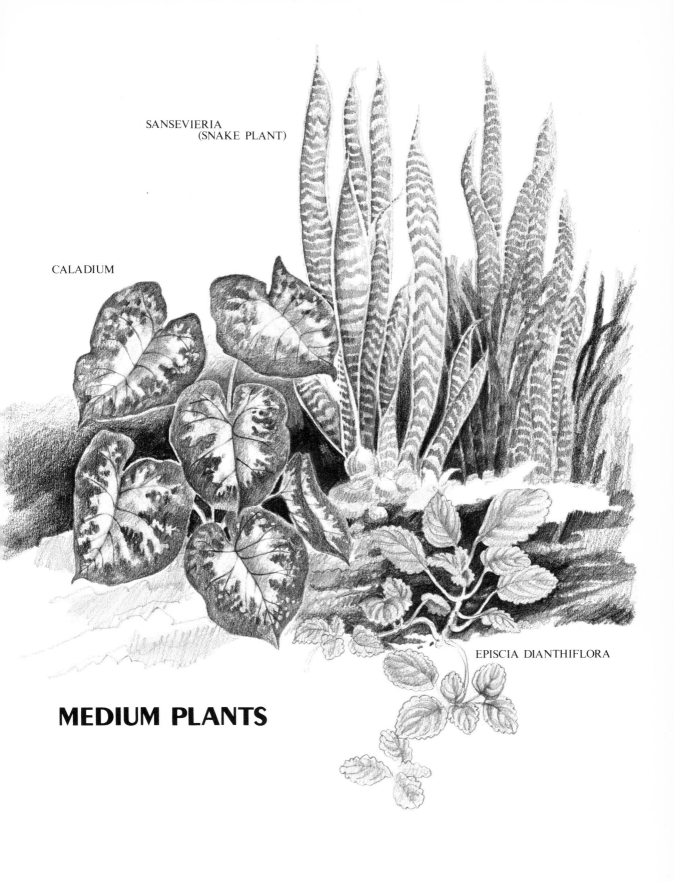

SANSEVIERIA
(SNAKE PLANT)

CALADIUM

EPISCIA DIANTHIFLORA

MEDIUM PLANTS

C. schmidtii A handsome plant, with red tinted leaves. Many other small species available. Use only in open terrariums. S; D

Cryptanthus bromeliodes tricolor One of the best small bromeliads, with rosettes of green leaves striped pink and white. *C. bivittatus (roseus picta)* bears bronze-pink foliage striped pale green.

C. acaulis (star plant) has bronze-green foliage, *C. terminalis* has bronze-green foliage, and *C. Beuckeri* has pale green foliage. All S; D or T

Ctenanthe oppenheimiana Dark green foliage with silver feathering. M; T

C. o. tricolor (rainbow plant) A rainbow of colorful foliage; good accent plant. Use in groups. M; T

Dizygotheca elegantissima (false arolia) Intricate scalloped leaves make this one desirable. Tough to grow. L; T

Dracaena godseffiana Slow-growing yellow- and green-leaved plant. Prune to keep small. L; T

D. goldieana Often sold, but not good for terrariums because it grows large quickly. L; T

D. sanderiana Deep green leaves lined white; rosette growth. Needs space. L; T

Euphorbia obesa (basketball plant) Grows to about 5 inches in diameter. A real curiosity: perfectly round gray-green ball with purple seams. S; D

Faucaria tigrina (tiger's jaw) An attractive gray-green plant spotted white; sometimes bears yellow flowers indoors. S; D

LARGE PLANTS

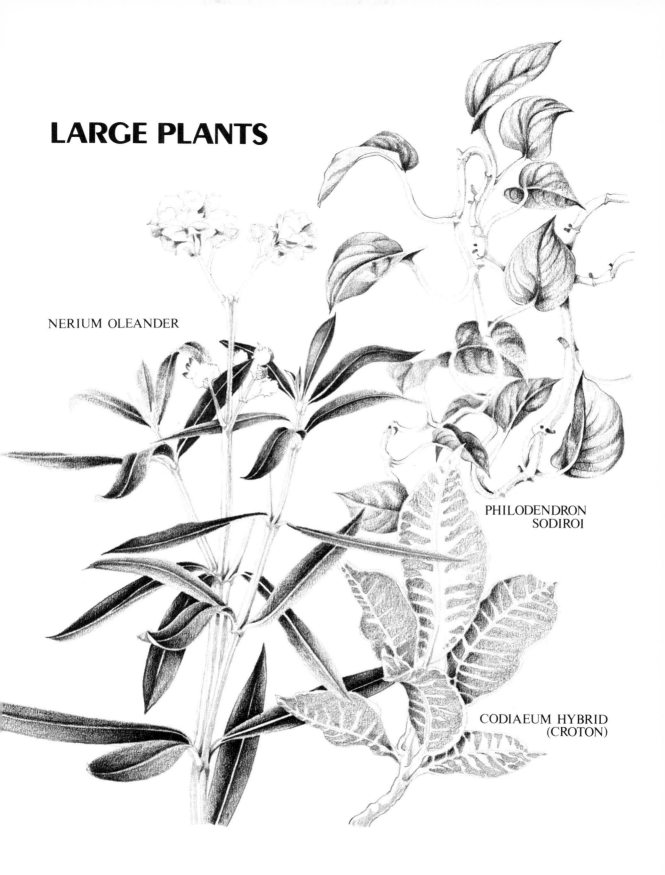

NERIUM OLEANDER

PHILODENDRON
SODIROI

CODIAEUM HYBRID
(CROTON)

Ficus radicans variegata Dainty foliage creeper; silver-green leaves marked white. Also desirable is *F. repens pumila* (creeping fig), with heart-shaped dark green foliage; sends out disks that cling to glass. Both S; W

Fittonia verschaffeltii (mosaic plant) A creeper, with iridescent foliage; grows slowly and remains dwarf size. Excellent. M; W

**Gasteria lilliputana* Thick stubby dark green leaves in a spiral pattern, mottled pale green. S; D

**Gymmocalycium mihanovichii* (chin cactus) Attractive and brightly colored; green with a red crown. S; D

Haworthia fasciata (zebra haworthia) A small plant, with dark green leaves banded crosswise with rows of white dots. S; D

H. tessellata Starlike rosette with sharp tip; stiff, dark green leaves lined with pale green. S; D

Hedera helix (ivy) Large group of delightful ivies; many are well suited for the glass garden. Try 'Buttercup'—golden yellow leaves; 'California Gold'—pale green leaves splashed yellow; 'Curlilocks'—apple-green leaves with ruffled edges; 'Glacier'—variegated triangular leaves; 'Needlepoint'—sharply cut leaves; and 'Pixie'—branching miniature ivy. All S; W

Hoya chaffa (miniature wax plant) Old favorite, with leathery glossy green leaves. S; T

Kleinia mandraliscae A fine species in an overlooked genus, with gray-green stems and finger-shaped leaves. S; D

K. repens (blue chalk sticks) Looks like its common name: blue-green cylindrical leaves in clusters. S; D

Malpighia coccigera (miniature holly) Glossy green leaves and pink flowers. Robust. M; W

Manettia bicolor (firecracker vine) Climbing vine that rarely fails to bear red and yellow flowers. After blooming, cut back to keep small. M; T

Maranta leuconeura kerchoveana (prayer plant) Low-growing plant with beautiful tapestry-colored leaves. Spectacular. Also try *M. l. massangeana*, with satiny bluish-green leaves reticulated with silver. Both M; T

Monanthes muralis A pretty, low-growing dwarf succulent. S; D

Muehlenbeckia nana (maidenhair vine) Mat-spreading creeper, with small dark green foliage. S; B

Myrtillocactus cochal Spiny bizarre branched cacti. Can grow large. M; D

Nerium oleander (oleander) Pink or white flowers on young plants. L; B

Pandanus veitchii (corkscrew plant) Striped yellow and green leaves; young plants are best. L; T

Pellionia repens Creeper with elliptical metal-green foliage; stays small. S; T

Peperomias Another group of excellent terrarium subjects, with decorative foliage. Leaf colors vary from greens to browns to maroon and variegated. Generally, plants stay low and bushy. All are S; T

P. bicolor Handsome olive-gray velvety leaves beautifully ribbed with silver.

(ABOVE) PEPEROMIA SANDERSII
A. PEPEROMIA VERSCHAFFELTII
B. PEPEROMIA NUMMULARIFOLIA
C. PEPEROMIA OBTUSIFOLIA MINIMA

PEPEROMIAS

P. caperata 'Emerald Ripple'   Heart-shaped emerald green leaves. Choice.

P. c. 'Little Fantasy'   Somewhat smaller form of *P. c.* 'Emerald Ripple.'

P. c. variegata   A variegated type of 'Little Fantasy.'

P. clusiifolia   Handsome metallic-green leaves with red margins. Excellent.

P. fosteriana   Dark green, rounded leaves. Lighter veins. Slow growing; good.

P. griseo argentea (ivy peperomia)   Quilted and thin silvery leaves with purple-olive veining. Grows in low rosette.

P. g. a. 'Blackie'   Blackish copper-green heart-shaped leaves. Low rosette. Choice.

P. incana   Erect wooly leaves.

P. marmorata 'Silver Heart'   Green and silver, heart-shaped leaves. Very decorative.

P. metallica   Small lanceolate bronzy leaves; small growing.

P. obtusifolia variegata (pepper face)   Light green and creamy white.

P. o. albo marginata minima   Grey-green with silver; dwarf.

P. ornata   Rosettes of silky green leaves with red ribs.

P. rubella   Whorls of small reddish leaves on red stems.

P. sandersii (watermelon peperomia) Silver and green striped leaf.

P. scandens Small cream and green leaves. Trailing.

P. verticillata Small hairy leaves in whorls.

Philodendron sodiroi One of the small philodendrons. Heart-shaped leaves. Keep trimmed. L; B

Pilea A vast group of fine terrarium plants, generally bushy and of the easiest culture. Leaf coloring varies from dark green to brownish green and to silver markings. Plants need a bright location (no direct sun) and average humidity to do their best. Trim occasionally to keep attractive. All are S; T

*P. cadierei minima (aluminum plant) Lovely tiny silvery leaves.

*P. depressa (miniature pilea) Tiny leathery leaves on creeping stems. Grows easily.

P. involucrata Deep brown leaves; somewhat hairy.

*P. nummulariifolia (creeping Charlie) Light green foliage on trailing stems.

*P. serpillacea A somewhat larger-growing Pilea.

*P. s. 'Silver Tree' Bushy, with bronze silvery leaves.

Plectranthus coleiodes (Swedish ivy) Light green scalloped leaves with white edges. Pinch and shape plant to desired size. L; T

Polyscias fruticosa elegans (ming tree) A delightful Aralia that looks like a ming tree. Lacy dark green foliage. M; W

(ABOVE) PILEA DEPRESSA
A. PILEA SERPILLACEA
B. PILEA SILVER TREE

PILEAS

PILEA INVOLUCRATA

PILEA NUMMULARIAEFOLIA

PILEA CADIEREI MINIMA

PILEAS

Rebutia kupperiana This small gray globe will produce myriads of red blooms. Only 2 inches across. S; D

R. minuscula (crown cactus) A lilliputian plant only a few inches around, with vibrant red blooms. S; D

Sansevieria (snake plant) Some varieties are low growing; ideal for the glass garden. Try 'Hahni'—a spiral of broad dark green leaves and 'Golden Hahni'—green leaves marked with yellow. M; W

Saxifraga sarmentosa (strawberry begonia) One of the best terrarium plants. A few inches high and slow growing. Excellent for gardens. Blackish-green lobed leaves. S; W

Scindapsus (Pothos) aureus (devil-ivy) Handsome heart-shaped leaves; keep pruned. M; B or T

Sedum Another group of plants with many diminutive gems. Most have small succulent leaves. Try *S. rubrotinctum, S. lineare, S. spurium,* or *S. confusum.* All S; D

Selaginella kraussiana brownii Creeping grass-green mossy plant. *S. uncinata* is another fine one, with blue-green tiny leaves. Both S; W

Sempervivum arachnoideum (cobweb houseleek) Gray-green rosettes of hairy leaves laced with silver webs. S; D

Syngonium (nephthytis) podophyllum Beautiful 8-inch plant, with arrow-shaped leaves. M; W

Tillandsia ionantha Tufted gem, with small rosettes of brilliant green leaves turning red at bloom time. S; D

Tolmiea menziesii (piggy-back plant) Bright green, somewhat hairy, leaves. Delicate grower not suitable for terrariums. Avoid. L; T

(ABOVE)   SEDUM RUBROTINCTUM
A. SEDUM LINEARE
B. SEDUM SPURIUM
C. SEDUM CONFUSUM

SEDUM

List of Flowering Plants

Achimenes

A large group of summer-flowering plants with open-faced blossoms and dark green leaves. Start rhizomes in spring. Fast grower; needs space. S; T

Allophyton mexicanum   Only 4 inches high. Dark green leaves; lavender and white flowers. Almost everblooming. S; T

Azalea 'Gumpo'   Delightful small variety, with frilly fire-red flowers. S; W; T

Begonias

This is a vast group of plants, but for terrariums we are interested only in the miniatures. And what delightful beauties these are! There is an incredible variety of leaf color to make a terrarium a veritable rainbow, and most of the miniatures delight in the warmth and humidity of closed containers. Here are just a few of the many to try (All are S; T):

B. aridicaulis.   Tiny green leaves, low growing.

B. boweri.   Old-time favorite, with bright green foliage and black stitched leaves.

B. 'Bow-Chance.'   Favorite small-leaved bright green hybrid.

B. 'China Doll'   A hybrid, with glistening green leaves, red stems.

B. dregei   Gnarled-type growth. Bronze-red maple-shaped leaves. Always good.

B. griffithi   A real exotic, with iridescent leaves.

A. BEGONIA
  WELTONENSIS

B. BEGONIA
  'CHINA DOLL'

BEGONIA 'BOW-CHANCE'

BEGONIAS

B. hydrocotylifolia   Round dark green leaves; attractive.

*B. 'Red Berry'   Wine-red Rex-type begonia.

*B. 'Red Wing' Wine red and silver leaves.

*B. 'Rosa Kugel'   A tiny wax begonia with small leaves.

B. rotundifolia   Apple-green foliage; handsome.

B. weltoniensis   Small, ovate 2-inch leaves, mapleleaf shape. Very pretty.

Bertolonia maculata   Miniature, with dark green, silver, and red foliage. Very appealing. S; T

Campanula (Bellflower)   Many varieties; mostly small plants with lovely white or blue flowers. M; W

Chrysanthemum multicaule (Chrysanthemum)   Bright yellow flowers; for a large case. M; T

Coleus rehneltianus (Coleus)   Highly colored plant that can be kept small by pruning; blooms with white flowers. L; T

Columnea hirta   Dark green hairy leaves and spectacular orange flowers. L; T

Crossandra infundibuliformis (orange glory)   Fine shiny green-leaved plant with crowns of orange flowers. Blooms young. M; T

Cyclamen coum   Favorite red-flowering plant, with dark green round leaves. S; W

Dianthus glauca nana   Not often seen, but satisfactory for the small glass garden. Bright pink flowers. S; T

Episcia dianthiflora   Velvety leaves of intense green; and white flowers. Small and dainty. M; T

Exacum affine   A gentian that bears blue flowers. M; T

Fragaria indica (Strawberry)   Small trailing plant with bright yellow flowers. Use with discretion; takes over a terrarium. S; W

Geranium (Pelargonium)

These lovely flowering plants are tough to resist because they are so beautiful. However, try them only after you have had some experience with terrarium gardening. Geraniums need coolness to thrive (55° F at night) and good ventilation, so remove terrarium covers at least once a day for a few hours. Here are some true small geraniums: (all are S; T)

'Aldebaran'—Dark pink flowers; leaves dark green zoned with blue-green.

'Altair'—Salmon pink flowers; intense green leaves. Lovely.

'Alycone'—Pink flowers; leaves 1½ inches in diameter. Bears flowers when only 2 inches tall.

'Antares'—Red flowers; rich black-green leaves. Handsome contrast.

'Capella'—Salmon-pink blooms; forest green foliage with darker markings.

'Filigree'—Salmon-pink blooms and fine tricolored foliage. Don't miss it.

'Goblin'—Double bright red flowers; compact. Good plant.

'Imp'—Pink flowers; dark foliage. Real tiny plant.

KLEINER LIEBLING VARIGATED

DWARF GERANIUM

KLEINER LIEBLING 'GREEN GOLD

PELARGONIUMS

'Kleiner Liebling'—Semi-dwarf dainty plant with fresh green leaves.

'Meteor'—Dark red double flowers; green foliage banded with black.

'Pigmy'—Bright red blooms; apple-green leaves. Rarely grows more than 6 inches tall.

'Red Comet'—Cherry red flowers with a white spot; foliage almost black-green.

'Ruffles'—Ruffled salmon-colored blooms; bears when only 2 inches tall.

Hypocyrta nummularia (goldfish plant)   Another fine gesneriad, with small shiny green leaves and pretty orange flowers. M; T

Impatiens   Look for dwarf variety 'Red Elfin,' with bright cheery flowers. S; W

Kalanchoe blossfeldiana   Many varieties; small red flowers. L; T

Kohleria amabilis   Silver-green leaves and tubular pink flowers. L; T

Orchids

Miniature orchids are plants that are made for terrarium growing. These 1- and 2-inch gems offer a wealth of flowers; the only special consideration is that you plant them in tree fern bark. Here are some good ones to grow. All S; T

Angraecum compactum   A miracle of nature, with leaves only 2 inches long and beautiful 2-inch white flowers.

ORNITHOCEPHALUS
IRIDIFOLIUM

ONCIDIUM PUMILUM

ORCHIDS

A. falcatum   One-inch bloom, with slender curved spurs. Strap-like dark green leaves.

Asconcentrum miniatum   Dozens of bright orange flowers to a plant.

Broughtonia sanguinea   Solitary green leaves only a few inches high. Branching scapes carry 1-inch brick-red flowers.

Bulbophyllum barbigerum   Produces an intricate flower with tufts of purple-brown hairs. Several blooms to a scape.

B. lemniscatoides   Has small, dark purplish flowers; the sepals have white hairs and a white and spotted red trailing ribbon appendage. A true oddity of nature.

B. morphologorum   A thrusting stem carries several hundred tiny yellow-brown flowers. Most unusual.

Cirrhopetalum cumingii   Tiny, to about 1 inch, with brilliant red and pink flowers in the shape of a half circle.

C. gracillum   Slender scapes that carry crimson-red flowers.

C. roxburghii   An umbrella of pink flowers; dark green foliage.

Masdevallia bella   About 10 inches tall. Bears a pendant scape with large triangular flowers; yellow sepals spotted red with dark tails.

M. caudata   About 5 inches high. The upper sepals are yellow spotted and veined red; lateral sepals are almost purple. Always desirable.

M. coccinea (M. harryana)   Clusters of glossy green leaves. The waxy flowers are about 4 inches long, ranging from pale yellow

Plastic sphere with woodland landscape. African violet is the center plant. (PHOTO BY MATTHEW BARR)

A handsome leaded glass terrarium house a miniature orchid and small rex begonia. (PHOTO BY MATTHEW BARR)

Ground covers and ferns grace this pyramid-shaped glass garden. (PHOTO BY MATTHEW BARR)

A lovely tropical garden thrives in this colorful parlor case. Plants are pileas, dracaena.
(PHOTO BY MATTHEW BARR)

This plastic cube (originally a light fixture) is home for dwarf evergreens.
(PHOTO BY MATTHEW BARR)

Here one lone miniature rose makes a dramatic statement in a dome garden.
(PHOTO BY MATTHEW BARR)

An elaborate leaded glass terrarium is used for a tropical landscape with assorted small house plants.

(PHOTO BY MATTHEW BARR)

Agloanema and pothos are the plants in this six-sided ornate case.
(PHOTO BY MATTHEW BARR)

A hand-blown bottle makes an excellent housing for fittonia and pilea.
(PHOTO BY MATTHEW BARR)

An old Swedish milk jar decorates a living room corner of the author's home. The scene created uses rocks and ledges and the plants are ferns and a croton.
(PHOTO BY MATTHEW BARR)

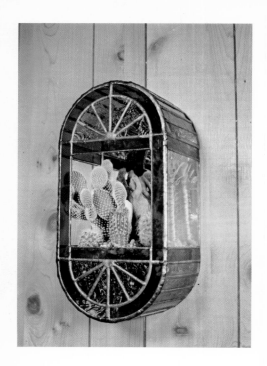

Desert gardens are always lovely; this one is in a wall terrarium of stained glass (Design, Richard Lee).
(PHOTO BY MATTHEW BARR)

A modernistic, many-sided terrarium duplicates a bog scene from nature with driftwood and low growing mosses and creepers (Design, Richard Lee).
(PHOTO BY MATTHEW BARR)

Hanging terrariums are lovely too; this is a leaded glass type with a tropical scene.
(PHOTO BY MATTHEW BARR)

*A slender glass vase can become a terrarium too;
here we see a tall pteris fern and fittonia.*
(PHOTO BY MATTHEW BARR)

Diminutive orchids live in this dome terrarium.
(PHOTO BY MATTHEW BARR)

*A five-gallon water bottle makes
a good terrarium; a flowering
plant in center is the accent.*
(PHOTO BY MATTHEW BARR)

*Desert gardens indeed look like
miniature landscapes; this geodesic
dome protects them from drafts
and maintains an even temperature for them.*
(PHOTO BY MATTHEW BARR)

A mushroom shaped terrarium has a variegated plectranthus and some moss as its residents. (PHOTO BY MATTHEW BARR)

An egg-shaped plastic terrarium is fine for tall plants; this one has a seedling maple in it. (PHOTO BY MATTHEW BARR)

The vertical woodland garden is well displayed in the Swedish milk jar. (PHOTO BY MATTHEW BARR)

Unusual bottles make good terrariums;
this one has a varied assortment
of house plants.
(PHOTO BY MATTHEW BARR)

A globe set on a dish makes this handsome
terrarium; plants are ferns and
small rex begonia at base. (PHOTO BY MATTHEW BARR)

LOWER LEFT. *Simplicity is the keynote*
here with one rex begonia in a glass vase.
(PHOTO BY MATTHEW BARR)

A tiny woodland landscape with rocks and stones and
varied plants are part of this mushroom terrarium.
(PHOTO BY MATTHEW BARR)

One of the newer terrarium shapes—
a plastic trapezoid. Note humidity control on top
(PHOTO COURTESY CHRISTEN INC.)

Square terrariums are eye appealing too; this one
also has humidity control on top
(PHOTO COURTESY CHRISTEN INC.)

This terrarium was made from a bottle garden kit
that comes with a stand
(PHOTO COURTESY CHRISTEN INC.)

through orange or scarlet to purple. Usually spring blooming, this is one of the easiest of the bunch to grow.

M. cupularis Glossy chocolate-spotted brown flowers. Easy to grow.

M. horrida Two-inch leaves and tiny greenish-yellow triangular flowers dotted with red. Blooms almost 6 months of the year.

M. ignea A handsome species, with a cinnabar-red flower striped crimson. The plant, 10 inches tall, has erect scapes, and most often blooms in spring for me. Popular and available.

Oncidium pumilum Small dark green leaves; dainty yellow flowers.

Ornithocephalus grandiflorus Erect scapes of pale green flowers.

O. inflexus About 5 inches high; tiny greenish-white flowers. Straplike foliage.

Pleurothallis chrysantha Radiant, with tiny burnt-orange flowers. Almost everblooming.

P. longissima A 9-inch plant, with erect scapes of whitish-yellow flowers.

Restrepia elegans Somewhat smaller than *R. antennifera*, but equally handsome. A superb 1- to 2-inch plant; bright flowers with a spoon-shaped lip.

Oxalis A fine group, with two excellent small species for glass gardens; *O. hedysaroides rubra*, with bright golden flowers, and *O. henrei*, with tiny yellow blooms. Both S; W

Punica granatum nana (dwarf pomegranate) Lovely small-leaved tree with red flowers. Prune and shape as desired. P. 'Chico' is good too. S; T or B

Rhipsalidopsis rosea Tiny and lovely; a fine cactus with rose-pink flowers. S; T or B

Rosa (Rose)
These diminutive replicas of their larger cousins are always desirable, and in small cool gardens they are elegant. Plants rarely grow more than 14 inches. Try these miniature roses for a stellar sight. All S; T

'Bo-Peep'—Lovely double pink flowers; prolific bloomer.

'Cinderella'—Old standby, with pink full flowers; likes coolness.

'Lilac Time'—Only 8 inches tall; bears splendid lilac flowers.

'Lollipop'—Fine variety, with splendid fiery red flowers.

'Midget'—Wee rose; small and fragrant; deep rose flowers.

'Pink Heather'—Blooms abundantly with double pink flowers.

'Pixie'—Well known and adored; tiny white flowers. Very small.

'Red Imp'—Intense red flowers make this one outstanding.

Saintpaulia (African Violet)
These have been favorites for years, and the miniatures make any glass garden glow with color. Some plants bloom on and off through the year with lavender, rose, or purple blooms. Plants will need some ventilation, so remove terrarium cover for a few hours a week. All are S; T

SAINTPAULIA 'DOLLY DIMPLE'

SAINTPAULIA SPECIES

SAINTPAULIA IONANTHA (PINK VARIETY)

SAINTPAULIAS

S. 'Dolly Dimple'—Deservable for its lovely blue flowers.

S. 'Honeyette'—Double red-lavender flowers. Only 5 inches.

S. 'Lavender Elfin Girl'—Ruffled and fluted foliage; lavender flowers.

S. 'Pink Rock'—Quilted leaves and single pink blooms.

S. 'Sweet Sixteen'—Double white flowers, scalloped spoon-shaped leaves.

S. 'Tinkle'—Fluted and ruffled foliage. Lavender blooms.

S. 'Tiny Bells'—Quilted dark green leaves; blue flowers.

S. 'Wendy'—Quilted leaves; large blue blooms.

S. 'White Doll'—Only 2 inches, with white flowers.

Schizocentron elegans (Spanish shawl)   Creeper, with tiny leaves and purple blooms. M; W, T

Sinningia pusilla   One of the finest miniatures. To 1 inch, with striking pink blooms. Not to be missed. Three varieties are available: 'Wood Nymph,' 'Dollbaby,' and 'Priscilla.' S; W or T

Streptocarpus   Gesneriads that offer a great deal of color for little effort. Try *S. rexii* (cape primore)—pale orchid flowers with purple throat, and *S. saxorum*—lavender-white blooms. M; W

Tillandsia ionantha   Charming tiny bromeliads with tufted leaves, bright purple flowers. S; D

Tradescantia multiflora   White flowers make this appealing. Will bloom in a bottle garden. S; T or B

6

MORE TERRARIUM PLANTS:
Ferns, Native Plants, and
Small Ground Covers and Mosses

We have discussed foliage and flowering house plants, including collector's plants such as begonias and orchids. Now we come to the delightful ferns, native plants, and small ground covers and mosses, plants that can be grown best in the protected environment of a terrarium. Try these plants after you have mastered a few gardens with the easier-to-grow foliage and flowering plants.

Ferns

Few plants can add as much beauty and grace to a terrarium as ferns. They are enchanting in translucent containers, where their delicate fronds glisten in early morning light. Ferns come in a myriad of different tones of green, from apple-green to dark, almost black-green. If you have had trouble growing tiny ferns at windows, do try them under glass. Ferns need a cool moist garden and enjoy the high humidity of a closed container. These plants must be positioned carefully so that they look natural rather than just stuck in place. Tuck them between rocks and ledges, and try to have fronds silhouetted against the inside walls of the container for a dramatic effect. There are hundreds of ferns, but here we list those that should never grow taller than 16 inches; most stay at about 10 inches, which is perfect for terrariums. *Note:* Plants in following lists (as in Chapter 5) are designated S, M, L, and W, B, D, or T after their descriptions.

PTERIS ENSIFORMIS VICTORIAE

PTERIS WILSONII

CYRTOMIUM FALCATUM

FERNS

Adiantum cuneatum gracillius (Maidenhair fern)   Small fern with very lacy emerald green fronds. Delicate and delightful plant. M; W or B

A. pedatum (American maidenhair)   Graceful curved fronds. Somewhat large. M; W

Asplenium platyneuron (Ebony spleenwort)   Feathery fronds and brown-purple stems. Large, but good. M; W

A. trichomanes (Maidenhair spleenwort)   A 6-inch fern with clustered fronds and 1-inch leaflets on black stems. M; W

Camptosorus rhizophyllus (Walking fern)   One of the best tiny ferns, with wedge-shaped leaves. S; B or D

Cyrtomium falcatum (Holly fern)   Somewhat large, but beautiful, with shiny toothed leaves. M; W

Davallia bullata mariesis (Rabbit-foot fern)   Creeping brown rhyzomes, lacy fronds. Select small plants; can grow large. M; B

This terrarium is predominantly planted with ferns; ground covers and mosses complete the landscape and a figurine adds dimension in the right corner.

Some excellent woodland mosses: club moss (left); shiny moss (center); and rainbow moss (right). (Photo by author)

Humata tyermannii   Small and delicate, very lacy fronds. Excellent, S; B

Microlepia setosa   Tiny delicate fern with feathery fronds. Good. S; B

Pellaea rotundifolia (Button fern)   Tiny button leaves of dark green on wiry stems. Choice terrarium plant. S; B or W

Polystichum tsus-simense   An old favorite. Wee feathery fern with great charm. S; T

Pteris cretica wilsonii (Table or brake fern)   Low and bushy crested fern. Stays small. Excellent. Many varieties. S; T

P. ensiformis victoriae (Silver lace fern)   Graceful with silver and green fronds. S; T or W

Native Plants

Our native greenery is nature's pure beauty, but many of the plants that once grew in the woods are becoming increasingly scarce. However, you can still grow them in the protected environment of a terrarium and have nature at your fingertips all year. The collecting of native plants is prohibited, but you can buy many wildflowers and ferns from suppliers (listed in Appendix E).

The natives are apt to be temperamental, and it might take them a while to get started in your glass garden. The main thing is that you can get them planted quickly and give them special attention the first few days. Watch to see how they are doing. If terrariums get too humid or there is too much moisture, open the lid daily. Once growing, the natives bring hours of countless pleasure. Included with the following group are the delightful native orchids:

Arisaema triphyllum (Jack-in-the-pulpit)   A charmer, with green striped spathes flushed with purple. Deciduous, difficult to grow, but will succeed in a large terrarium that is very airy and cool. M; B

Cypripedium acaule (pink ladyslipper)   Pink and lovely, but it needs a strongly acid soil. M; W or B

C. parviflorum   This is the orchid you should try because it will succeed in a cool moist terrarium with slightly acid soil. It bears a fragrant yellow flower atop a 12-inch stem. M; W or B

C. pubescens   Yellow flowers; large grower. M; W

Chimaphila maculata (striped pipsissewa)   Arrow-shaped leaves with lovely veining. S; W or B

NATIVE PLANTS

STRIPED PIPSISSAWA

GOLD THREAD

TRAILING ARBUTUS

Coptis trifolia (goldthread)   A dainty plant with handsome scalloped leaves. S; B

Dionaea muscipula (Venus flytrap)   A curious insect-eating plant. Small, with bright green claw foliage. An oddity. S; B

Drosera rotundifolia (sundew)   A unique plant that is fascinating to watch: tiny round leaves with hairy blades that capture insects. S; B

Epigaea repens (trailing arbutus)   Bright green leaves and white or pink flowers. Needs a very acid soil to survive. S; W or B

Goodyera pubescens (rattlesnake plaintain)   A dainty plant, with oval green leaves veined white. S; W

Hepatica acutiloba (sharp-leaved liverleaf)   Three-lobed leaves; flowers may be white or pink. Grows in neutral soil and probably will be the first in the terrarium to bloom in spring. M; B

Mitchella repens (partridge berry)   An evergreen creeper that bears red berries at Christmas and lasts for many weeks. M; W

Pyrola elliptica   Sometimes called wintergreen; a 3-inch leaved plant with white flowers. Grows to 10 inches. S; B

Sanguinaria canadensis (bloodroot)   A gray-green plant that likes shade. Has white, early spring flowers. M; W

Trillium grandiflorum   Bears lovely white flowers with pink hues and grows to 18 inches. L; W

T. undulatum   Has white flowers with a rosy throat. L; W

Viola canadensis   Lovely little wild plant with purple blooms. S; W, B

Small Ground Covers and Mosses

Small ground covers and mosses are indispensable in glass gardens because they clothe the soil with verdant green and offer grace; they are the finishing touches to the terrarium. Essentially, ground covers are outdoor plants, sold at nurseries. (You can not buy mosses but you can grow your own, as discussed in the next chapter.) Many will adapt to the conditions of a glass container, provided they have constant moisture and shade.

Ground covers are larger plants than mosses. It is wise not to use too many of them, but a few patches of baby's tears or Scotch moss add a wealth of green color to a terrarium.

Most mosses for terrariums come from the Rhodobryum, Mnium, Climacium, Bryum, and Timmia families. Use mosses in *woodland*

Looking into a terrarium we see a woodland scene with pitcher-plants and rattlesnake plantain. (Photo by author)

A Venus flytrap and a seedling maple are the occupants of this plastic terrarium. Ground cover is in the rear. (Photo by Matthew Barr)

and *bog* gardens, which are naturally shady and moist. They will grow on soil, wood, or stone. Once established they should grow for some time. Besides looking well, mosses serve a valuable function in a glass container because they soak up excess water, thus preventing a stagnant situation.

Mosses must be planted immediately. To plant, push tiny pieces in place in the soil. Be sure they are well inserted. If they just rest on top they will soon die.

The subject of mosses is enormous, and if you want to delve further read the delightful book *Forests of Lilliput* by John Bland (Englewood Cliffs, N.J.: Prentice-Hall, Inc., 1972). (See Appendix D).

Here are some ground covers to try in your terrariums:

Alyssum wulfenianum   Low and compact, with grayish foliage.

Anthemis nobilis (chamomile)   Lovely narrow leaves. Grows easily and smells good too.

Arenaria verna caespitosa (Irish moss)   Yellow-green vibrant color; a favorite.

Asperula odorata (sweet woodruff)   Grows somewhat tall, to about 8 inches. Fragrant.

Helxine soleirolii (baby's tears)   Popular, with tiny dark green leaves. Use with caution because it spreads quickly.

Mentha requienii (Carsican mint)   Small leaves. A fine green accent.

Nepeta hederacea (ground ivy)   Round- or kidney-shaped leaves; do not confuse with English ivy.

Sagina subulata (Scotch moss)   Lovely, dense mat. *S. subulata* 'Aurea' is golden green.

Sedum (many kinds)   Several small-leaved species; mostly button leaves that are dark green or brown-green.

Thymus (thyme)   Many species. Small leaves. Good creeper.

Veronica repens   Creeping mosslike plant with tiny leaves.

7

WHERE TO GET PLANTS
And How to Grow Your Own

When I first started terrarium gardening I could rarely find plants I really wanted; miniatures were scarce, and specialty plants like orchids and begonias were almost unavailable. Today growers have responded with gusto to the demand for small plants; hundreds are available. You can buy plants from mail-order suppliers, local nurseries, florists, house plant sections of patio and department stores, Woolworth stores, and even supermarkets. Thus, the selection is vast, and choosing the right plants deserves careful consideration. Most but not all plants will grow in a terrarium, so it is wise to know something about plants and where to get them before you start your small gardens. You can also start or get many plants for little cost by sowing seed, using cuttings or divisions, or trying plantlets (offsets from mature plants).

Mail Order

Mail-order companies, listed in garden magazines, offer a great assortment of miniature plants, ranging from African violets to orchids. For example, Merry Gardens of Maine has a splendid selection of small ferns, Arthur Allgrove in Delaware has a comprehensive list of woodland miniatures, and Hauserman Orchids in Elmhurst, Illinois, has a fine selection of diminutive species. (For more sources see Appendix E).

Order all plants by air, even if it costs more, and have them shipped in their original pots rather than out-of-pots (bare-root). If shipped bare root, plants take longer to regain their vigor. When you receive plants, inspect them to see if they have insects. An easy way—and one I have used for years—is to sink the pots to the rim in a sink of water for an hour; any unwelcome guests will surface.

Do not immediately unpot your plants and put them in their new homes. Let them grow in their original containers for a few days. Once they have regained vigor they can then be removed and placed in the terrarium.

If possible, order plants in spring and fall because summer heat kills plants quickly, and extremely cold winter weather is hazardous and can harm plants. When you order, order sufficiently. You may think ten plants are enough, but once in a terrarium they may seem like little. I use at least a dozen plants for a 12-inch glass garden.

Nurseries and Florists

Nurseries that specialize in outdoor plants carry some house plants, including a few miniatures, but they stock mainly seedlings such as philodendron and dizygotheca, which can be quite tall when mature. Prices are moderate and selection fair. Quality as a rule is superior, and you rarely get a bad plant. However, few nurseries label their plants with proper names, and I have yet to find attendants who recognize plants by name (if they do at all). Yet all in all these are good places to buy plants.

Florists invariably have a very limited supply of small house plants because they specialize in seasonal pot plants and want to sell planted terrariums rather than only the plants, so it is best—as a rule—to avoid the large florist. It simply does not make sense to pay 5 dollars for a house plant to put in a terrarium when it is available elsewhere in a smaller, much cheaper version.

Patio and Department Stores

House plant centers in patio and department stores (they have improved vastly in recent years) are where you can find a good selection of plants. Not all will be miniatures, and not all will be properly labeled, but the price is right, and plants are generally fresh and healthy. Some stores will have plants with common names only; you can look up their botanical names in the back of this book in Appendix C.

Woolworths and other similar stores now have a large array of good terrarium plants at moderate prices. This is where I buy a great many plants. The assortment in recent months has been very good, and you will be able to find some really good glass-garden subjects. Of course, not every Woolworths has the same buyer, and the selection may not be as good in one place as in another, but I have checked three Woolworths in San Francisco with excellent results. In Chicago, I also found a fine selection, but at Woolworths in New York there was only a fair choice when I was there.

House Plant Boutiques

Recently, a new kind of plant shop has appeared on the American scene. This is a specialized business with house plants as the main feature. You can find a great many fine terrarium subjects, including miniature plants. These establishments are a welcome addition to the garden picture because they fill the gap between the nursery (which does not specialize in house plants) and the florist (who does not stock too many) and the department store plant sections. Furthermore, the owners of these shops are generally well informed about indoor plants and can answer many of your questions about care.

In addition to a fine selection of plants, the stores also carry terrariums and all necessary supplies and will, if asked, plant your terrarium or one you buy from them. And perhaps the most outstanding feature of the new plant boutiques is that prices are fair. There is no exorbitant markup of merchandise, so all in all the customer gets a fair deal. Look for these stores in your area. I have seen them in Chicago, Los Angeles, New York, St. Louis, and San Francisco.

Grow Your Own

You can grow house plant seeds in almost any container whether bought or from your household items, especially kitchen containers. For example, coffee cans and aluminum pans that frozen rolls come in are ideal. The squatty azalea type pot sold at nurseries makes another good container. Note that any household item must be at least 3 to 4 inches deep and have some drainage holes.

Use any suitable sterile growing medium (peat, vermiculite, perlite, or a packaged seed-starter), making sure it is firm, dense, and moist. Fill the containers with the mix to within a half inch from the top. Now press the mixture into place so there are no air pockets. Place seeds ½ inch apart. Fine-type seed can be merely scattered on top of the mix, but cover large and medium seeds with a layer of dry growing medium that is twice the thickness of the seed. Moisten the top of the growing medium. Now use a Baggie on sticks to make a tent, and cut or punch a few air holes in it so too much moisture does not accumulate inside the homemade propagating case. Put the containers in a bright area (but no direct sun), and make sure the spot has daytime temperatures of 65° to 75° F. and a nighttime drop of about 10°. Never let the seed bed get soggy; it should be moist. When you see tiny leaves sprouting, germination has occurred. Now is the time to remove the Baggie so seedlings can get more air. Move the containers to a brighter window (again, no direct sun).

Never let the medium dry out; check it daily. Move containers to very bright light when you see the second set of leaves. Transplant seedlings to pots of soil when they are about 1 inch high and have separate leaves, lifting them carefully with a blunt-nosed tool, getting as much of the rootball as you can. Feed lightly; in a few more weeks you can plant your seedlings in your terrariums.

Ferns require a different procedure because they develop from spores (minute specks on the back of the fronds), not seeds. Tap spores off on a sheet of paper when they are dry (and they *must* be dry). Use milled sphagnum moss to sow spores, and always keep them moist with ample humidity. Cover the containers with glass or plastic. Ferns must have warm temperatures, with a minimum of 70° F. for ideal germination. Spore germination takes 3 to 5 weeks; the true ferns will grow from the first green growths (*prothallis*). When this occurs, remove glass or plastic covers. After all true leaves are up transfer the tiny ferns to terrariums.

You can get new plants from old ones by removing offsets, suckers, or runners. These growths are tiny plants that emerge from the base of mature plants. Remove and pot them individually when they are 2 to 3 inches tall. In about a month they will be ready for terrarium planting.

Division is still another method of getting new plants: separate mature plants that have several crowns. Run a sterile knife through the crowns and then pot the crowns one to a container. In a month or so they will be ready for your terrarium.

Starting Your Own Mosses

As mentioned, you will not be able to buy mosses from nurseries. You can transplant them from the wild, but the best way is to start your own plants. This is not difficult but it does take time.

You will find natural mosses on stones, wood, or in soil in shady wild habitats. Take shallow squares (you will not need much), and dry them on a newspaper or cardboard. When they are dry, remove the green part of the mosses by crumbling away old soil. The fine dry moss will be your "starter" for your own mosses.

Take the dried moss and put it in a soil-and-peat bed in a shallow tray. (You can use any household throwaway such as milk cartons or aluminum dishes that rolls come in.) Insert a layer of cheesecloth over the soil and sprinkle the dried "starter" on top. Cover this with another layer of cheesecloth and water lightly but thoroughly with a mister. The cheesecloth should always be moist to the touch. Put the moss in a shady place, with temperatures about 72° to 78° F. In about 2 months moss should start growing; in another month the moss is ready for your terrariums. Slice it as you would a cake, and then insert the wedges on soil or stones.

8

CREATING THE GARDEN

A garden in glass can be made in 10 minutes or 10 hours; what you create depends entirely on your imagination and talent. The first gardens I did many years ago were merely assemblages of plants placed haphazardly in a container. The plants lived and thrived, but the resulting picture was hardly aesthetically pleasing.

Creating the miniature greenery is just as important as planning your outdoor garden, although the scope is, of course, much smaller. The scene should be pleasing to the eye in texture, color, and arrangement. There should be no jarring notes because everything miniature gets *close* scrutiny. So why not take the extra time and make a fine garden instead of an ordinary one?

It is easier to recreate a scene you remember from nature. Think back to that woodland visit when you were a child, and perhaps simulate this picture. Or if you have been in the desert, make a tiny slice of that landscape in your terrarium. If the tropical jungle has always been your favorite, follow this plan. With a theme, you will find that gardening in small containers becomes a pleasure; you are no longer dealing with only plants but nature as well.

General Planning and Planting Techniques

Do you remember those walks in the country years ago? The scene that appealed to you most was probably one with hills and valleys rather than a flat terrain. So in your terrariums vary the contour of the soil. Fashion hills and create valleys, but do it carefully. There is a difference between a mound of soil and a hill—you will need a careful eye. If necessary, work from a photograph. The idea is to create a center of interest—a rocky ledge, the side of a hill—and to

90

pLANTiNG THE TERRARIUM

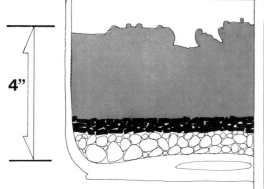

4"

FUNNEL IN GRAVEL, CHARCOAL, AND SOIL.

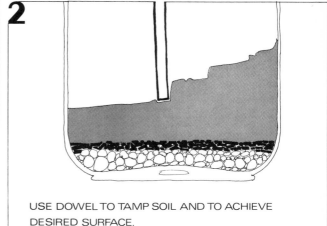

2

USE DOWEL TO TAMP SOIL AND TO ACHIEVE
DESIRED SURFACE.

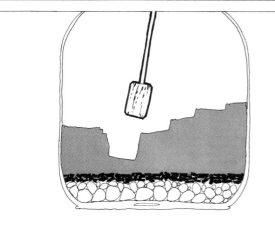

MAKE HOLE WITH TOOL.

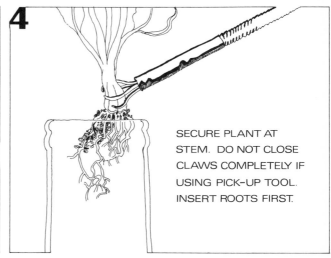

4

SECURE PLANT AT
STEM. DO NOT CLOSE
CLAWS COMPLETELY IF
USING PICK-UP TOOL.
INSERT ROOTS FIRST.

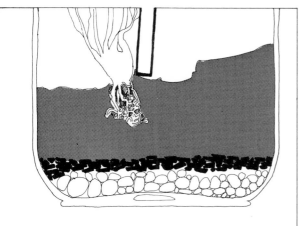

TAMP SOIL AROUND ROOT OF PLANT.

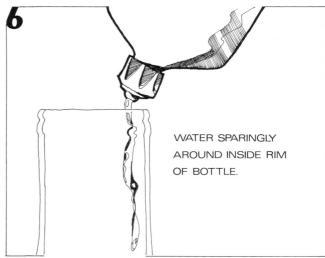

6

WATER SPARINGLY
AROUND INSIDE RIM
OF BOTTLE.

Planting the plastic sphere: soil and rocks in place. (Photo by Matthew Barr)

Positioning plants. (Photo by Matthew Barr)

The completed terrarium. (Photo by Matthew Barr)

allow a slope to the front of the container. This way the eye will travel from the center of interest to the front of the bowl or from the front to the rear. Do take time with the original landscaping and change it as you go if the first design does not please you.

To start the garden be sure the container is scrupulously clean. Avoid detergents or windowspray solution; use soap and water, and rinse thoroughly several times. After you dry the container, spread the gravel on the bottom of the terrarium; use a little less than one-fourth the height of the container. Sprinkle in some charcoal chips, enough to cover the gravel bed. Now add soil, to about one-fourth the height of the container. Some gardeners say that the soil should be moist, but I have used soil as it comes from the package with success for years and doubt that moist soil adds anything to the planting; all it does is muddy your hands.

I have found that small rocks placed intelligently can be used with great success. Fill around the rock with soil, leaving a few edges showing, and you will accomplish an interesting peak. If the container allows it, use one large rock and two smaller ones filled in and around with soil. Try it; you will see the difference immediately.

Now select the plants for the scene (see Appendix B and Chapters 5 and 6). Each group of plants should be appropriate for the picture you want to create: woodland, tropical, and so forth. Remove the small plants (miniatures preferably) from their pots by tapping the pot against the side of a table and coaxing the plant from its container. To do this, grasp the crown of the plant between your thumb and finger and loosely jiggle it. It should come out with the root intact. Crumble away some (but not all) soil, and set the plant in place in predug planting holes. Firm around the collar of the plant with soil so there are no air gaps. (For bottle gardening you will have to remove all soil and wash roots and then allow plants to dry).

Place taller plants in the rear or to one side as accents. Then work forward, locating shorter plants in front of the tall ones. In the rear use large-leaved plants. In front concentrate on diminutive-leafed

planting plan for the square

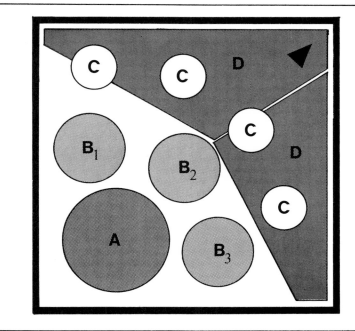

PLANT KEY

A LARGE

B MEDIUM

C SMALL

D GROUND COVER

PLANT NAMES

A CHAMAEDOREA
ELEGANS

B$_1$ AGLAONEMA
COMMUTATUM

B$_2$ DRACAENA
SANDERIANA

B$_3$ PLECTRANTHUS
COLEOIDES

C IMPATIENS,
BEGONIA(S),
GERANIUM(S),
ARDISIA CRENATA

D OXALIS,

varieties. Try to achieve variation in leaf sizes, working from large to medium to small or from small to medium to large. This will accomplish a rhythm pleasing to the eye and add dimension to the garden. Avoid placing a large-leaved plant next to a tiny-leaved one because this jars the eye and ruins the illusion.

All plants of the same green color can be monotonous, so use gradations: dark green to medium green to apple green. Avoid abrupt changes. A yellow-leaved plant next to a dark green one is disconcerting, so mix and match carefully to gain the beauty a well-planted terrarium gives.

The above rules are general. There are always exceptions, such as planting both sides of the container with tall plants, which creates a formal but handsome picture. There is no accent, just a mirror image reminiscent of Victorian gardens.

If you decide not to do an assimilated nature scene and want to use only a few plants, select those with sculptured stems and leaves much like bonsai planting. The focus is the plant, which must be perfect in every respect.

If you decide to use variegated-leaved plants, by all means do so, but carefully. Too many colors can ruin the effect of a terrarium. If you use variegated plants, use a group as an accent rather than a single one that will appear out of place.

Techniques for Variously Shaped Containers

SQUARE: These gardens need vertical plants like acorus and palms. Place the plants to one side, never in the center. Fill the center area with smaller plants and low-growing mosses. Avoid bushy or rosette-type spreading plants because the curves of the foliage will fight with the lines of the container. Use tree-type plants, and cluster smaller plants around them. By all means do leave some open area; a cube filled with plants will look unattractive.

OCTAGONAL AND HEXAGONAL: These containers are fun to plant because there is generally more space and corners for in-

planting plan   OCTAGONAL

PLANT KEY
A LARGE
B MEDIUM
C SMALL

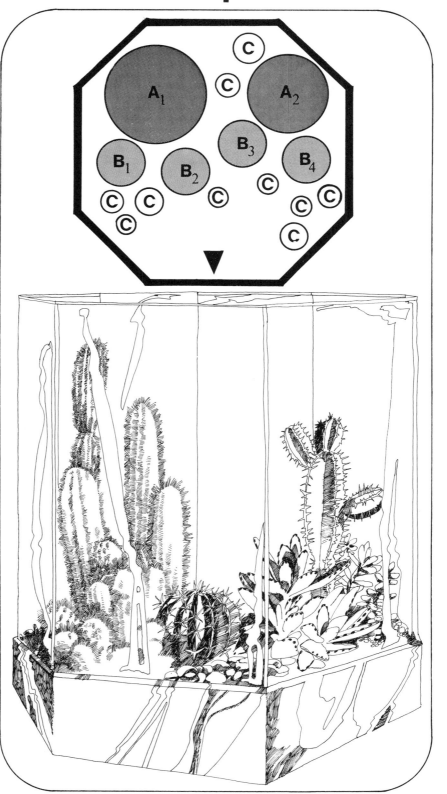

PLANT NAMES

A_1 CLEISTOCACTUS STRAUSSII

A_2 MYRTILLO-CACTUS

B_1 MAMMILLARIA

B_2 LOBIVA

B_3 KALANCHOE

B_4 SEDUM

C ROCK SUCCULENTS

Planting the cube container. Note dish glued to bottom to hold in soil.
(Photo by Matthew Barr)

Positioning plants. (Photo by Matthew Barr)

The finished terrarium. (Photo by Matthew Barr)

terest. Avoid one center of interest; use several to create a handsome picture. Octagonal and hexagonal terrariums are usually larger than most, so many, many plants can be used; for example, two dozen plants would not be too many.

CIRCULAR (Dome and Globe): When we talk of domes we mean the glass bells used in Victorian times. The domes need suitable circular dishes on which to rest. The newer globe shape (like a light bulb design) also relies on the circular planting dish. The dome is relatively easy to plant; for best results choose a large one, say 12 inches in diameter (anything less limits the planting). Because of the height of the dome, generally 12 to 16 inches, you can use tall plants with ease. But select plants with graceful delicate leaves. Use one or two such plants—*Polyscias fruticosa*, for instance—as the accent, and then fill in and around with smaller plants following the arc arrangement, with the center open for viewing. Do not try to cram in too many plants; keep the design simple and elegant, like the dome itself.

Planting the dome terrarium. (Photo by Matthew Barr)

planting plan dome

PLANT KEY

A LARGE
B MEDIUM
C SMALL
D GROUND COVER

PLANT NAMES

A SYNGONIUM

B₁ ANTHURIUM
SCHERZERIANUM

B₂ CHLOROPHYTUM
BICHETII

B₃ CHAMAERANTHE-
MUM IGNEUM

C BEGONIA
BOWERI

D OXALIS

planting plan   sphere

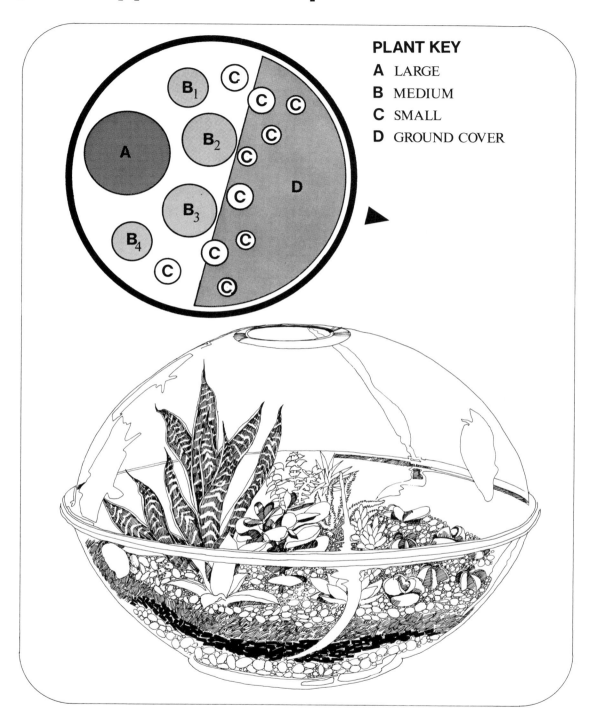

PLANT KEY

A LARGE
B MEDIUM
C SMALL
D GROUND COVER

PLANT NAMES

A SANSEVIERIA TRIFASCIATA

B_1, B_2, B_3 CRASSULA

B_4 ECHEVERIA

C HAWORTHIAS; SEDUMS

D LITHOPS;
   ASTROPHYTUM

The globe shape, although circular too, is generally limited to a 10-inch planting-area dish. Restraint is the best procedure. Use a few tall plants for accent, with only two or three smaller plants around them.

RECTANGULAR: This design requires a similar planting plan as for the square terrarium. However, the rectangular container has more lateral planting space. Put the main plant to one side of the container—left or right (never in the center)—and use lower-growing plants around it to form an island effect. To balance the scene, put another planting group on the other side (in the rear), but do not make it as dominant as the original accent. In other words, the plants should not be as tall. To bridge the two accent islands, plant small-leaved sprawling plants; use several, not just one. By following this arc arrangement you will have a lovely scene, with the front open for viewing.

A trapezoid-shaped terrarium has recently appeared on the market. This is essentially a rectangle with four flared sides. The planting plan for this new design remains very much the same as for the rectangle, although more branching plants can be used to follow the contours of the trapezoid shape.

BOTTLE GARDENS: The same planting *rules* apply, but planting *procedure* is different.

Fill bottle with 3 to 4 inches of soil and charcoal through a funnel.

Insert a dowel or blunt-edge stick, and make planting holes. If the soil is not damp, moisten the tip of the stick.

Clean plant thoroughly of soil, and run it under water. Allow plant to dry a few hours, or blot it on newspaper.

Place the crown of the plant in planting tool (pickup tool or looper).

Push roots first through neck of bottle, and lower the plant into depression.

When plant is in hole, carefully slip away the planting tool.

planting the long neck

1 Funnel in gravel, charcoal, potting soil.

2

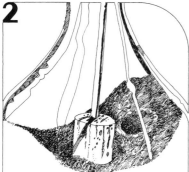

Tamp and shape soil for desired surface; Make planting holes.

3

Use coat hanger with loop shaped at end to secure plant as shown.

4

Place dowel gently on root stock to hold plant in place; remove wire tool by passing stem through loop opening.

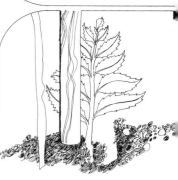

Push soil around plant and tamp gently.

Use long-snouted watering container to water around inside rim of bottle.

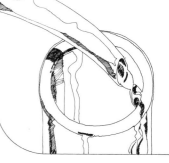

Close-up photos of planting plan of verticle glass jar. (Photo by Matthew Barr)

While doing this you might have to support the plant with the dowel stick.

Firm the soil with the dowel.

Clean neck of bottle because dirt may have accumulated. Use the planting tool with a wad of Kleenex at end.

Run a scant bit of water along rim of the bottle, and let it trickle into soil. Tip bottle to one side to clean the inside as water runs down. Remove soil from leaves with a brush on a stick.

There are a few tricks that can make the garden outstanding. I believe that clothing the soil completely in mosses or gravel is the secret. Use low-growing mosses liberally. If you can not find true moss (and they are scarce), use ground covers such as Irish moss or Chamomile or any small-leaved creeping plant. (Ground covers and mosses were discussed in Chapter 6.)

9

MAINTENANCE OF TERRARIUMS

All plants need some care, and plants in terrariums are no exception. Although it is true that many miniature landscapes can go untended for weeks, those with special plants will need some special care. Removing dead blossoms and twigs are necessary precautions against disease and insect invasion; and grooming keeps plants in scale with the total landscape.

Also observe plants for signs of illness. If they appear limp and wan, there is something wrong. Perhaps they need a different environment, for example, woodland instead of tropical. If leaves turn brown for no reason, insects or soggy soil could be the causes. If foliage appears brown at edges, the soil may be accumulating too much toxic salts, in which case transplanting is necessary.

Grooming, Insect Protection, Disease

Grooming and removing dead and decayed leaves, stems, and flowers is absolutely necessary to keep terrarium gardens in good health. If left to remain, these decayed parts can help bring on fungus and bacterial diseases that will quickly ruin a small greenery. Then, once plants are weakened, insects may invade the greenery.

For bottle gardens you will need an X-acto cutting knife (at artists' stores) or at least a dowel with a single-edged razor blade attached to it to get into small openings. Cut away decayed parts, and remove them with a long-handled tweezer attached to a dowel stick. (Attach the implement with rubber bands or Scotch tape). Or remove parts with a pickup tool.

If the soil becomes covered with fungus or mold, remove it carefully, and apply fresh soil. Do not wait until disease or fungus really gets a start; watch and observe and take action quickly.

Trimming an overgrown terrarium; the plants had been in the glass dome for about a year. (Photo by Matthew Barr)

You will rarely find insects in closed terrariums because there is little chance of them getting in, but occasionally red spider, aphids, or white flies may appear. Generally, I think these bugs hatch some time after plants are in the terrarium (at least this is the only way I can figure that they get in). If you see crawling insects, try to identify them before you take action:

1. APHIDS—green, black, pink, or red sucking insects.
2. MEALYBUGS—look like cottony white clumps. Usually found under leaves and near leaf axils.
3. RED SPIDER—diminutive mites impossible to see but their webs are usually visible.
4. THRIPS—almost invisible yellow, brown, or black sucking insects.
5. WHITE FLY—look like tiny little moths.
6. SCALE—insects with hard or soft shells, about $\frac{1}{8}$-inch across.

You will find most insects on the undersides of leaves or in leaf axils, so these are the places to watch. Rather than use poisons in the home, first try some old-fashioned remedies that I believe work well. Make a solution of laundry soap and water: use 1 teaspoon of soap to 1 quart of water, and spray plants thoroughly (use a window-cleaning spray bottle). Then rinse plants with clear warm water. Repeat this operation twice a week until insects are eliminated. Or use alcohol on cotton swabs to remove mealybugs and aphids. If these methods are too tedious and time consuming, try an insecticide, but do use one that is nonpersistent and nonaccumulative in the soil. Buy plant remedies that are derived from botanicals, such as rotenone, quassi, pyrethrum, and ryannia. These are now being made by commercial manufacturers, and they are the safest to use at home.

Most plants will tolerate insecticides, but some, such as orchids, cacti and succulents, and palms will not. They can be harmed by strong chemicals. For these plants, stick to the old-fashioned remedies mentioned.

The terrarium plants are now trimmed and garden is ready for the dome. Dome is at left. (Photo by Matthew Barr)

Occasionally a plant may get a heavy infestation of insects, for example, if you are away on vacation. Should this happen, remove the plant and dispose of it rather than jeopardize other plants in the garden.

More serious perhaps than insects in a terrarium are fungus or bacterial diseases. If fungus does appear, and you will see this in the form of gray or brown mold on leaves or stems (soil, too), apply a light solution of a fungicide such as Captan. If you object to poisons in the home, use some powdered sulfur (available at nurseries) or charcoal. Remove infected leaves or stems, and then dust wounds with the remedy. Heavy moisture coupled with dark days are invitations for fungus to start so, as mentioned, keep terrariums in a bright place.

Plant Cures And Clues

Sometimes plants simply do not grow well in a terrarium, even with the best care. This may be because they are (1) planted too deeply or too shallowly; (2) they are weak to begin with; (3) they are not able to adjust to new conditions, or (4) they are being crowded by stronger plants. So before you blame insects, see if the plant has been properly planted. If everything seems well but the plant does not grow, remove it and try a different one.

Plants, like people, give clues if they are not satisfied with their surroundings:

1. Leaves turn yellow—plants are getting too much moisture.
2. Leaves drop off—the foliage may be touching the glass.
3. Leggy growth—plants are not getting enough light.
4. Foliage shows brown or black blotches—the plants are getting too much sun.
5. Leaf tips turn brown—excess moisture is the problem.
6. Salts deposit on the glass—hard water may be the cause. Let water stand overnight.

7. Leaves develop small brown or discolored red spots—icy water on the foliage may be the cause.

Repairing a Terrarium

Occasionally a terrarium may break if it is glass or crack if it is plastic. This may mar the total effect of the garden, but you need not discard the greenery. Modern epoxies make glass repairing simple and take only a few minutes; adhesives are also available for fixing plastic cracks or crazes. Above all, keep the inside and outside of the glass perfectly clean. Use warm soap and water solution on a cloth, and avoid cleaners that contain ammonia, or cleansers that will mar and scratch the surfaces.

What To Do When Plants Get Too Big

Invariably, after a time, unless you have used true miniatures, plants in terrariums will outgrow their homes. With some plants this may occur in 2 years, but others may last for 5 or more years. The point is, do not discard the plant or just leave it in the terrarium; remove (repot), trim, or separate it to make new plants.

Redoing a terrarium is at times necessary too; this is a complete redecorating job with new soil, new plants, and so forth. It is not difficult, and where once you had one type of greenery, now you can change the scene with little effort.

Repotting, Trimming, and Separating Plants

The word repotting is a misnomer because all you have to do is merely remove the plant and replace it with another. The process is simple: Scoop out the root ball with the plant and then repot in individual containers. Prepare the new pot as follows: put in some pot pieces over the drainage hole, and add a sprinkling of stone and charcoal and a mound of soil. Center the overgrown plant, and fill

This bottle garden is overgrown after two years and plants are being removed with a pickup tool. (Photo by Matthew Barr)

Always remove plants root first with leaves at bottom; then plant can be repotted in container for windowsill growing. (Photo by Matthew Barr)

in around it with fresh soil. Pat soil down to eliminate air pockets, and then water thoroughly.

If the terrarium plant has become a favorite of yours, and you want to keep it in the glass garden, trim away ungainly, too-tall stems and cut it to scale. This may seem cruel, but I assure you that it does not harm the plant. Indeed, it will branch and send out new shoots in a short time. If the plant is a crown-type grower you can merely remove one of the crowns to make a new plant (pot up in soil), and leave the other one in the case. It is best to remove fast-growing plants entirely. Otherwise, you will have to trim them back radically every 3 months.

Redoing

If a terrarium becomes terribly overgrown and no longer looks attractive, it might be wise to redo the entire landscape with fresh plants and a new scene. To do this, remove the lid or cover, and let the soil dry out somewhat. Take out the plants, being careful to save those you might want to replant. Now, with a stick, crumble the soil and discard it. Wash the container—glass bowl, dome and tray, bottle, whatever—with a soap and water solution. Rinse well with warm water until everything is crystal clear. Dry thoroughly and start your new terrarium.

This is the time to remember the mistakes you might have made in the first setting. Use more care and more discretion about plants you choose. Remember our words about tall and small growers, little-leaved plants and bold ones, foliage color, and so forth (Chapter 8). Take your time and create the perfect slice of nature that is your very own.

10

TERRARIUMS FOR KIDS

If you have had trouble getting your children interested in indoor gardening, give them an empty container and some plants and see what happens. They will be absorbed for hours; unlike a plant at the window, which they are apt to pass by and not notice, the diminutive scene offers the young a world of enchanting beauty.

For years I tried to figure out what would interest children in the way of gardening. Recently, at a library lecture about terrariums, I found that half my audience were children. They were wide-eyed and excited over these little green worlds in glass.

Whether it is the aspect of having a garden of their own in a glass globe or seeing a complete tiny scene they can handle that attracts them I am not sure, but children do adore terrariums. Once you teach them the basics they will go at it themselves and create gardens that will boggle your imagination.

Containers and Props

Use inexpensive goldfish bowls or similar containers (bubble bowls rather than exotic cases) for children's terrariums. Children are familiar with these objects, and because little hands get cut easily, the bowls with smooth surfaces lessen the chances of cuts, as does an aquarium with its protective aluminum moldings.

Supply the kids with stones and gravel, or let them collect their own seashells and the like. Part of the fascination of terrarium gardening is using all sorts of things to create the landscape. Children are natural collectors of stones, marbles, and other paraphernalia that can find a place in a glass garden. Let them create complete scenes rather than only a few plants in a container. Give

116

A terrarium such as this is fine for kids; it allows them easy access to plant-ing. Let the children create diminutive landscapes rather than just put plants in haphazardly. (Photo by Matthew Barr)

them easy-to-grow plants (see list at end of chapter) and unique ones such as Venus flytraps or prayer plants. Do not interfere with their plant arrangements, although perfect they will not be. You will be amazed at how quickly they will realize their mistakes and correct them, for example, when a plant is too large for a terrarium. Let them learn by doing; do not do it for them.

Plants

Plants that grow quickly or ones that do something (sundew, Venus flytrap) intrigue kids. If they use such plants (and you should let them), the little garden may become smothered with foliage in a few months. But then you can show them how to take it apart and use the plants elsewhere. As children plant their terrariums, point out plant common names to stimulate interest rather than letting them just put plants in place.

Even the most well-intentioned child will eventually find plants of his own, perhaps snatched from your garden. Do not panic. Experimentation is part of the fun, and soon he or she will realize that an outdoor plant will not survive long in a terrarium. Then the child will start asking questions and get more and more interested in plants.

If by chance you find a frog or lizard included in the terrarium, all the better. Little creatures do live in little green worlds, and the vivarium—a place for plants and animals—is a wonderful way to introduce your child to nature. The small animals are busy in the little garden in their daily activities and provide hours of fascinating viewing. You will find the plant-and-pet garden a blessing on those rainy days when children can not be outdoors (see end of chapter for pet list for terrariums).

Keeping It Going

If at first your child does not succeed in making the terrarium a fit place for plants, do not do it for him; have him try it again.

In the author's terrarium a small lizard perches on top of a rock (center). Kids love gardens with small creatures and this is an ideal way for them to find interest in plants and animals. (Photo by author)

Once the garden starts growing, he will be intrigued and stay with it. For children's terrariums, some grass seed or tiny bulbs will provide quick results and get the young interested.

As mentioned, let the child use unusual plants like oxalis or the prayer plant (Maranta) that fold their leaves at night. Put in Venus flytraps and pitcher plants that trap insects for food. Children are fascinated by these oddities.

Also try growing fern spores in the terrarium; this is easily done on a stone or brick if the terrarium is kept quite humid. Or for even faster results, sprinkle seeds of beans, lentils, peas, and so forth. These sprout quickly, grow fast, and need only some sphagnum moss to germinate. Let the kids grow some moss in their terrarium

(as outlined in Chapter 6), that you can then use in your own terrariums. This is an excellent way of making a child feel helpful and of getting him to participate in a project.

In the proper season, snip some flowering shrub branches and let the kids force them into bloom in their terrarium. In a matter of a few days colorful blossoms will sprout for the enjoyment of everyone in the family.

Easy-to-Grow Plants for Children's Terrariums:

Spider plant *(Chlorophytum bichetii)*
Devil ivy *(Scindapsus (Pothos) aureus)*
Prayer plant *(Maranta leuconeura kerchoveana)*
Aluminum plant *(Pilea cadieri minima)*
Sundew plant *(Drosera rotundifolia)*
Venus flytrap *(Dionaea muscipula)*
Walking fern *(Camptosorus rhizophyllus)*

Small Animals for Terrariums:

Horned toads
Tree frogs
Wood frogs
Salamanders

This Victorian terrarium houses two lizards and several tropical plants.

APPENDIX

A: Terrarium Plants
        Small
        Medium
        Large
B: List of Plants
        Woodland
        Bog
        Desert
        Tropical
C: Common Names of Plants
D: Books to Read
E: Where to Buy Plants
F: Where to Buy Terrariums

Appendix A
TERRARIUM PLANTS
Small (to 10 inches)

Achimenes
Acorus gramineus pusillus (sweet flag)
Adromischus clavifolius
A. maculatus (calico hearts)
Allophyton mexicanum
Aloe brevifolia variegata
Alternanthera bettzichiana
Angraecum compactum
A. falcatum
Ascocentrum miniatum
Astrophytum myriostigma (bishop's cap)
Azalea 'Gumpo'
Begonia aridicaulis
B. 'Bow Chance'
B. boweri
B. 'China Doll'
B. dregei
B. griffithi
B. hydrocotylifolia
B. 'Red Berry'
B. 'Red Wing'
B. 'Rosa Kugel'
B. rotundifolia
B. weltoniensis
Bertolonia maculata
Broughtonia sanguinea
Bulbophyllum barbigerum
B. lemniscatoides
B. morphologorum

Calathea bachemiana
C. picturata argentea
Camptosorus rhizophyllus (walking fern)
Chimaphila masculata (striped pipsisewa)
Cirrhopetalum cumingii
C. gracillimum
C. roxburghii
Coptis trifolia (goldthread)
Cotyledon
Crassula cooperi
C. schmidtii
Cryptanthus acaulis (star plant)
C. Beuckeri
C. bivittatus (roseus picta)
C. bromelioides tricolor
C. terminalis
Cyclamen coum
Dianthus glauca nana
Dionaea muscipula (Venus flytrap)
Drosera rotundifulia (sundew)
Epigaea repens (trailing arbutus)
Euphorbia obesa (basketball plant)
Faucaria tigrina (tiger's jaw)
Ficus radicans variegata
F. repens pumila (creeping fig)
Fragaria indica
Gasteria lilliputana
Geranium 'Aldebaran'
G. 'Altair'
G. 'Alycone'
G. 'Antares'
G. 'Capella'
G. 'Filigree'
G. 'Goblin'
G. 'Imp'

G. 'Kleiner Liebling'
G. 'Meteor'
G. 'Pigmy'
G. 'Red Comet'
G. 'Ruffles'
Goodyera pubescens (rattlesnake plantain)
Gymnocalycium mihanovichii (chin cactus)
Haworthia fasciata (zebra haworthia)
H. tessellata
Hedera helix 'Buttercup'
H. h. 'California Gold'
H. h. 'Curlilocks'
H. h. 'Glacier'
H. h. 'Needlepoint'
H. h. 'Pixie'
Hoya chaffa (miniature wax plant)
Humata tyrmannii
Impatiens
Kleinia mandraliscae
K. repens (blue chalk sticks)
Masdevallia bella
M. caudata
M. coccinea (harryana)
M. cupularis
M. horrida
M. ignea
Microlepia setosa
Oncidium pumilum
Ornithochilus grandiflorus
O. inflexus
Oxalis hedysaroides rubra
O. henrei
Pellaea rotundifolia (button fern)
Pellionia repens
Peperomia bicolor

P. caperata 'Emerald Ripple'
P. c. 'Little Fantasy'
P. c. variegata
P. clusiaefolia
P. fosteriana
P. griseo argentea (ivy peperomia)
P. g. a. 'Blackie'
P. incana
P. marmorata 'Silver Heart'
P. metallica
P. obtusifolia variegata (pepper face)
P. o. albo marginata minima
P. ornata
P. rubella
P. sandersii (watermelon peperomia)
P. scandens
P. verticillata
Pilea cadierei minima (aluminum-plant)
P. depressa (miniature pilea)
P. involucrata
P. nummulariifolia (creeping Charlie)
P. serpillacea
P. s. 'Silver Tree'
Pleurothallis chrysantha
P. longissima
Polystichum tsus-simense
Pteris cretica Wilsonii (table fern)
P. ensiformis Victoriae
Punica granatum nana (dwarf pomegranate)
Pyrola elliptica (shinleaf)
Rebutia kupperiana
R. minuscula (crown cactus)
Restrepia elegans
Rhipsalidopsis rosea
Rosa 'Bo Peep'

R. 'Cinderella'
R. 'Lilac Time'
R. 'Lollipop'
R. 'Midget'
R. 'Pink Heather'
R. 'Pixie'
R. 'Red Imp'
Saintpaulia 'Honeyette'
S. 'Dolly Dimple'
S. 'Lavender Elfin Girl'
S. 'Pink Rock'
S. 'Sweet Sixteen'
S. 'Tinkle'
S. 'Tiny Bells'
S. 'Wendy'
S. 'White Doll'
Saxifraga sarmentosa (strawberry geranium)
Sedum confusum
S. lineare
S. rubrotinctum
S. spurium
Selaginella kraussiana brownii
S. uncinata
Sempervivum arachnoideum (cobweb houseleek)
Sinningia pusilla
S. p. 'Dollbaby'
S. p. 'Priscilla'
S. p. 'Wood Nymph'
Tillandsia ionantha
Tradescantia multiflora
Vicia canadensis
V. pedata

Medium (to 18 inches)

Adiantum cuneatum gracillius (maidenhair fern)
A. pedatum (American maidenhair)
Aglaonema commutatum (Chinese evergreen)
A. pictum
Anthurium scherzerianum (flamingo plant)
Arisaema triphyllum (Jack-in-the-pulpit)
Asplenium platyneuron (ebony spleenwort)
A. trichomanes (maidenhair spleenwort)
Bambusa nana (miniature bamboo)
Caladium humboldtii
C. h. 'Little Rascal'
C. h. 'Twilight'
Campanula (bellflower)
Ceropegia cafforum (string of hearts)
C. woodii (rosary vine)
Chamaeranthemum igneum
Chlorophytum bichetii (spider plant)
Chrysanthemum multicaule (chrysanthemum)
Crossandra infundibuliformis (orange glory)
Ctenanthe oppenheimiana
C. o. tricolor (rainbow plant)
Cypripedium acaule (pink ladyslipper)
C. parviflorum
C. pubescens
Cyrtomium falcatum (holly fern)
Davallia bullata mariesis (rabbit-foot fern)
Episcia dianthiflora (tapestry plant)
Exacum affine
Fittonia verschaffeltii (mosaic plant)
Hepatica acutiloba (sharp-leaved liverleaf)
Hypocyrta nummularia (goldfish plant)
Malpighia coccigera (miniature holly)
Manettia bicolor (firecracker vine)

Maranta leuconeura kerchoveana (prayer plant)
M. l. massangeana
Mitchella repens (partridge berry)
Monanthes muralis
Muehlenbeckia nana (maidenhair vine)
Polyscias fruticosa elegans (ming tree)
Sanguinaria candensis (bloodroot)
Sansevieria (snake plant)
Schizocentron elegans (Spanish shawl)
Scindapsus (pothos) aureas (devil's ivy)
Streptocarpus rexii (cape primrose)
S. saxorum
Syngonium (nephthytis) podophyllum

Large (over 18 inches)

Chamaedorea elegans (bamboo palm)
Codiaeum variegatum pictum (croton)
Coleus rehneltianus (coleus)
Columnea hirta
Dizygotheca elegantissima (false avalia)
Dracaena godseffiana
D. goldieana
D. sanderiana
Kalanchoe blossfeldiana
Kohleria amabilis
Nerium oleander (oleander)
Pandanus veitchii (corkscrew plant)
Philodendron sodiroi
Plectranthus coleiodes (Swedish ivy)
Tolmiea menziesii (piggy-back plant)
Trillium grandiflorium
T. undulatum

Appendix B
LIST OF PLANTS

WOODLAND TERRARIUMS: need cool and moist conditions; shady location. Do best in closed cases with high humidity, say 70 to 80 percent. This is a cool verdant greenery.

Acorus gramineus pusillus (sweet flag)
Adiantum cuneatum gracillius (maidenhair fern)
A. pedatum (American maidenhair)
A. trichomanes (maidenhair spleenwort)
Alyssum wulfenianum
Asplenium platyneuron (ebony spleenwort)
A. trichomanes (maidenhair spleenwort)
Azalea 'Gumpo'
Calathea bachemiana
Campanula (bellflower)
Chimaphila maculata (striped pipssisewa)
Cyclamen coum
Cypripedium parviflorium
C. pubescens
Cyrtomium falcatum (holly fern)
Ficus radicans variegata
F. repens pumila (creeping fig)
Fittonia verschaffeltii (mosaic plant)
Fragaria indica (strawberry)
Hedera helix (ivy)
Helxine soleirolii (baby's tears)
Impatiens
Malpighia coccigera (miniature holly)
Maranta leuconeura kerchoveana (prayer plant)
Mitchella repens (partridge berry)
Oxalis hedysaroides rubra
O. henrei

Polyscias fruticosa elegans (ming tree)
Sanguinaria canadensis (bloodroot)
Sansevieria (snake plant) (many kinds)
Saxifraga sarmentosa (strawberry geranium)
Schizocentron elegans (Spanish shawl)
Selaginella kraussiana brownii
S. uncinata
Sinningia pusillus
S. p. 'Dollbaby'
S. p. 'Priscilla'
S. p. 'Wood Nymph'
Streptocarpus rexii
S. saxorum
Syngonium (nephthytis) *podophyllum*
Trillium grandiflorum
T. undulatum
Veronica repens
Viola canadensis
V. pedata

BOG TERRARIUMS: Need moist, shady, and cool conditions. Soil should always be wet to the touch. Must be in no sun at all.

Alyssum wulfenianum
Arisaema triphyllum (Jack-in-the-pulpit)
Camptosorus rhizophyllus (walking fern)
Coptis trifolia (goldthread)
Davallia bullata mariesis (rabbit-foot fern)
Dionaea musipula (Venus flytrap)
Drosera rotundifolia (sundew)
Hepatica acutiloba (sharp-leaved liverleaf)
Humata tyrmannii
Microlepia setosa
Philodendron sodiroi
Pyrola Elliptica (shinleaf)

Selaginella kraussiana brownii
Syngonium podophyllum
Viola canadensis (violet)

DESERT TERRARIUMS: Need warmth and dryness, with cooler temperatures at night. Grow the desert scene in a partially open container; in closed cases plants will rot from excessive moisture. Some sun is suitable but not too much. Always try to keep terrarium well ventilated.

Aloe brevifolia variegata
Adromischus clavifolius
A. maculatus (calico hearts)
Astrophytum myriostigma (bishop's cap)
Cleistocactus strausii
Cotyledon
Crassula arborescens
C. cooperi
C. schmidtii
Euphorbia obesa (basketball plant)
Faucaria tigrina (tiger's jaw)
Gasteria lilliputana
Gymnocalycium mihanovichii (chin cactus)
Haworthia fasciata (zebra haworthia)
H. tessellata
Kleinia mandraliscae
K. repens (blue chalk sticks)
Monanthes muralis
Myrtillocactus cochal
Rebutia kupperiana
R. minuscula (crown cactus)
Sedum confusum
S. lineare
S. spurium
S. rubrutinctum

Sempervivums (houseleek) (many kinds)
Tillandsia ionantha

TROPICAL TERRARIUMS: Need warmth and some sun and coolness at night. These landscape scenes can tolerate some sunshine, but be sure to remove cover or lid a few hours a day for best results. Soil should be moist but never soggy.

Aglaonema commutatum (Chinese evergreen)
A. pictum
Allophyton mexicanum
Angraecum compactum
A. falcatum
Anthurium scherzerianum (flamingo plant)
Ascocentrum miniatum
Azalea 'Gumpo'
Begonia aridicaulis
B. 'Bow Chance'
B. boweri
B. 'China Doll'
B. dregei
B. griffithi
B. hydrocotylifolia
B. 'Red Berry'
B. 'Red Wing'
B. 'Rosa Kuqel'
B. rotundifolia
B. weltoniensis
Broughtonia sanguinea
Bulbophyllum barbigerium
B. lemniscatoides
B. morphologorum
Caladium
Chamaedorea elegans (bamboo palm)
Chamaeranthemum igneum

Chlorophytum bichetti (spider plant)
Cirrhopetalum cumingii
C. gracillimum
C. roxburghii
Crossandra infundibulformis (orange glory)
Cryptanthus bromelioides tricolor
Ctenanthe oppenheimiana
Dizygotheca elegantissima (false aralia)
Dracaena godseffiana
D. goldieana
D. sanderiana
Episcia dianthiflora
Geraniums (all miniature or dwarf types)
Hypocyrta nummularia
Kalanchoe blossfeldiana
Masdevallia bella
M. caudata
M. coccinea (harryana)
M. cupularis
M. horrida
M. ignea
Oncidium pumilum
Ornithocephalus grandiflorus
O. inflexus
Pellionia repens
Peperomia bicolor
P. caperata 'Emerald Ripple'
P. c. 'Little Fantasy'
P. c. variegata
P. clusiaefolia
P. fosteriana
P. griseo argentea (ivy peperomia)
P. g. a. 'Blackie'
P. incana
P. marmorata 'Silver Heart'

P. metallica

P. obtusifolia variegata (pepper face)

P. o. albo marginata minima

P. variegata

P. ornata

P. rubella

P. sandersii (watermelon peperomia)

P. scandens

P. verticillata

Pilea cadierei minima (aluminum plant)

P. depressa (miniature pilea)

P. involucrata

P. nummularifolia (creeping Charlie)

P. serpillacea

P. s. 'Silver Tree'

Plectranthus coleiodes

Pleurothallis chrysantha

P. longissima

Polystichum tsus-simense

Pteris cretica wilsonii (table fern)

P. ensiformis victoriae

Restrepia elegans

Rosa (rose) (all miniature types)

Saxifraga sarmentosa (strawberry geranium)

Schizocentron elegans (Spanish Shawl)

Sinningia pusilla

Tolmiea menzensii (piggy back plant).

Appendix C
COMMON NAMES

African violet (*Saintpaulia*)
aluminum plant (*Pilea cadierei minima*)
American maidenhair (*Adiantum pedatum*)
baby's tears (*Helxine soleirolii*)
bamboo palm (*Chamaedorea elegans*)
basketball plant (*Euphorbia obesa*)
bellflower (*Campanula*)
bishop's cap (*Astrophytum myriostigma*)
bloodroot (*Sanguinaria canadensis*)
blue chalk sticks (*Kleinia repens*)
button fern (*Pellaea rotundifolia*)
calico hearts (*Andromischus maculatus*)
cape primose (*Streptocarpus rexii*)
chamomile (*Anthemis nobilis*)
chin cactus (*Gymnocalycium mihanovichii*)
Chinese evergreen (*Aglaonema commutatum*)
chrysanthemum (*Chrysanthemum multicaule*)
cobweb houseleek (*Sempervivum arachnoideum*)
coleus (*Coleus rehneltianus*)
corkscrew plant (*Pandanus veitchii*)
Corsican mint (*Mentha requienii*)
creeping Charlie (*Pilea nummulariaefolia*)
creeping fig (*Ficus repens pumila*)
croton (*Codiaeum variegatum pictum*)
crown cactus (*Rebutia minuscula*)
devil ivy (*Scindapsus (pothos) aureus*)
dwarf pomegranate (*Punica granatum nana*)
ebony spleenwort (*Asplenium platyneuron*)
false aralia (*Dizygotheca elegantissima*)
firecracker vine (*Manettia bicolor*)
flamingo plant (*Anthurium scherzerianum*)

goldfish plant (*Hypocyrta nummularia*)
goldthread (*Coptis trifolia*)
ground ivy (*Nepeta hederacea*)
holly fern (*Cyrtomium facatum*)
Irish moss (*Arenaria verna caespitosa*)
ivy (*Hedera helix*)
ivy peperomia (*Peperomia griseo argentea*)
Jack-in-the-pulpit (*Arisaema triphyllum*)
maidenhair fern (*Adiantum cuneatum gracillius*)
maidenhair spleenwort (*Asplenium trichomanes*)
maidenhair vine (*Muehlenbeckia nana*)
ming tree (*Polyscias fruticosa elegans*)
miniature bamboo (*Bambusa nana*)
miniature holly (*Malpighia coccigera*)
miniature pilea (*Pilea depressa*)
miniature wax plant (*Hoya chaffa*)
mosaic plant (*Fittonia verschaffeltii*)
oleander (*Nerium oleander*)
orange glory (*Crossandra infundibuliformis*)
partridge berry (*Mitchella repens*)
pepper face (*Peperomia obtusifolia variegata*)
piggy-back plant (*Tolmiea menziesii*)
pink ladyslipper (*Cypripedium acaule*)
prayer plant (*Maranta leuconeura kerchoveana*)
rabbit-foot fern (*Davallia bullata mariesis*)
rainbow plant (*Ctenanthe oppenheimiana tricolor*)
rattlesnake plantain (*Goodyera pubescens*)
rosary vine (*Ceropegia woodii*)
rose (*Rosa*)
Scotch moss (*Sagina subulata*)
sharp-leaved liverleaf (*Hepatica acutiloba*)
Shinleaf (*Pyrola elliptica*)
silver lace fern (*Pteris ensiformis victoriae*)
snake plant (*Sansevieria*)
Spanish shawl (*Schizocentron elegans*)

spider plant (*Chlorophytum bichetii*)
star plant (*Cryptanthus acaulis*)
strawberry begonia (*Saxifraga sarmentosa*)
string of hearts (*Ceropegia cafforum*)
striped pipsissewa (*Chimaphila maculata*)
sundew (*Drosera rotundifolia*)
swedish ivy (*Plectranthus coleiodes*)
sweet flag (*Acorus gramineus pusillus*)
sweet woodruff (*Asperula odorata*)
table fern (*Pteris cretica wilsonii*)
thyme (*thymus*)
tiger's jaw (*Faucaria tigrina*)
trailing arbutus (*Epigaea repens*)
Venus flytrap (*Dionaea musipula*)
walking fern (*Camptosorus rhizophyllus*)
watermelon peperomia (*Peperomia sandersii*)
zebra haworthia (*Haworthia fasciata*)

Appendix D
BOOKS TO READ

All About Miniature Plants and Gardens, Bernice Brilmayer, Doubleday & Co., 1963

All About House Plants, Montague Free, Doubleday & Co., 1946

Bottle Garden and Fern Cases, Anne Ashberry, Hodder & Stoughton, 1964

Cacti and Succulents, Indoors and Out, Martha Van Ness, Van Nostrand Reinhold, 1971

Garden In Your House, A, Ernesta Drinker Ballard (Rev. Ed) Harper & Row, 1972

Gardens Under Glass, Jack Kramer, Simon & Schuster, 1969

Growing Orchids At Your Windows, Jack Kramer, Hawthorne Books, 1972

Miniature Plants, Elvin McDonald, D. Van Nostrand, 1966

Miniature Flower Arrangements & Plantings, Lois Wilson, Hawthorn Books, Inc., 1963

The Joy of Geraniums, Helen Van Pelt Wilson, Wm. Morrow & Co., 1971

Miniature Rose Book, Margaret E. Pinney, D. Van Nostrand Publishers, 1964

Pets and Plants in Miniature Gardens, Jack Kramer, Doubleday and Co., 1973

PAMPHLETS AND PERIODICALS

Audubon Nature Bulletin. series 4, no. 1, The Terrarium

Audubon Nature Bulletin. series 16, no. 8, "Adventures with Wild Plants, Indoors & Out."

Brooklyn Botanic Gardens, Plants & Garden Series, Autumn, 1968, "Miniature Gardens". $1

Appendix E
WHERE TO BUY PLANTS

Alberts & Merkel Bros., Inc.
2210 S. Federal Hwy.
Boynton Beach, Fla. 33435

Orchids, tropical plants. Catalogs 50 cents

Arthur Eames Allgrove
Box 459
Wilmington, Mass. 01887

Unusual selection of many terrarium plants. Catalog free

Barrington Greenhouse
860 Clemente Rd.
Barrington, N.J. 08016

Miniature house plants of many kinds. List.

Buell's Greenhouses
Eastford, Conn. 06242

Gloxinias, other gesneriads. Catalog $1

W. Atlee Burpee Co.
Philadelphia, PA 19132

House plants, seeds. Catalog free

Cactus by Mueller
10411 Rosedale Hwy.
Bakersfield, Calif. 93307

Many kinds of cacti. Catalog 10 cents

Cook's Geranium Nursery
712 N. Grand
Lyons, Kansas 67554

Miniature geraniums. Catalog 25 cents

Craven's Greenhouses
4732 W. Tennessee
Denver, Colo. 80219

African violets, other gesneriads.

Fischer's Greenhouses
Dept. HC
Linwood, N.J. 08221

Gesneriads and foliage house plants. Catalog 50 cents

Hausermanns Orchids
Box 363
Elmhurst Ill. 60128

Many kinds of small orchids. Catalog free

142

Henrietta's Cactus Nursery
1345 N. Brawley
Fresno, Calif. 93705

Large selection of cactus & succulents. Catalog 20 cents

Ilgenfritz, Margaret Orchids
Monroe, Michigan 48161

Large selection of miniature orchids. Catalog $1

Kartuz Greenhouses
92 Chestnut St.
Wilmington, Mass. 01887

Gesneriads, and begonias. Catalog 25 cents

Leslie's Wildflower Nursery
30 Summer St.
Methuen, Mass. 01884

Wildflowers; catalog.

Logee's Greenhouse
55 North St.
Danielson, Conn. 06239

Begonias, gesneriads, various house plants. Catalog 50 cents

Lyon, Lyndon
14 Multcher St.
Dolgeville, N.Y. 13329

African violets, other house plants. Price list.

Merry Gardens
Camden, Maine 04843

Huge selection of house plants. Catalog $1

Mc Combs' Greenhouses
New Straitsville, Ohio 43766

Varied house plants.

Geo. W. Park Seed Co.
64 Cokesbury Rd.
Greenwood, S.C. 29646

Good selection of house plants. Catalog free.

Plant Oddities
Box 127
Basking Ridge, N.J. 07920

Carnivorous plants. Catalog 25 cents

Savage Gardens
P.O. 163
McMinnville, Tenn. 37110

Woodland terrarium plants. List available.

Tinari Greenhouses
2325 Valley Rd.
Huntington Valley, Pa. 19006

African violets, other gesneriads. List.

Appendix F
WHERE TO BUY TERRARIUMS

Terrariums, plastic or glass, are in variety, department, and gift stores all over the country. Vases and bottles of all kinds are also at department stores and gift shops. Pet shops have an assortment of unique aquariums that can be used as terrariums too.

However, for people not in metropolitan areas, here is a list of mail-order suppliers of terrariums. Also included are manufacturers of terrariums; these companies do not sell retail but if you write them, they will advise you of their dealers.

Arthur E. Allgrove
North Wilmington, Mass.
01887

Plastic domes and glass terrariums.

Anchor Hocking Corp.
1099 Broad St.
Lancaster, Ohio 43130

Glass candy jars and other containers. No retail. (Write for dealers)

B. L. Designs
354 Manhattan Ave.
Brooklyn, N.Y. 11211

Dome and bottle terrariums. No retail. (Write for dealers)

Christen Inc.
59 Branch St.
St. Louis, Mo. 63147

Plastic and glass terrariums. No retail. (Write for dealers)

Crystal Glass Tube
& Cylinder Co.
7310 S. Chicago Ave.
Chicago, Ill. 60619

Glass domes of all kinds.

Hobby-Time
783 Harding St.
Minneapolis, Minn. 55413

Knocked-down terrarium kits.

House Plant Corner   Plastic terrariums.
Box 165 S
Oxford, Maryland 21654

New Renaissance Glass Works   Knocked-down leaded glass
5636 College Ave.   kits.
Oakland, Calif. 94618

Nichols Herb and Seed Co.   Plastic terrariums.
1190 N. Pacific Hwy.
Albany, Oregon 97321

Raja Toy Co.   Plastic domes and kits.
1206 La Jolla Ave.
Los Angeles, Calif. 90035